MEDIA CANARDS

iUniverse, Inc.
New York Bloomington

iUniverse books may be ordered through booksellers or by contacting:

iUniverse
1663 Liberty Drive
Bloomington, IN 47403
www.iuniverse.com
1-800-Authors (1-800-288-4677)

Because of the dynamic nature of the Internet, any Web addresses or links contained in this book may have changed since publication and may no longer be valid. The views expressed in this work are solely those of the author and do not necessarily reflect the views of the publisher, and the publisher hereby disclaims any responsibility for them.

ISBN: 978-1-4401-5958-9 (sc)
ISBN: 978-1-4401-5959-6 (ebook)

Printed in the United States of America

iUniverse rev. date: 03/12/2010

Ca-nard

Pronunciation: \kə-'närd\

1 a : a false or unfounded report or story ; especially **:** a fabricated report **b :** a groundless rumor or belief

CONTENTS

PROLOGUE
1

CHAPTER ONE
How The Media Became Dishonest
5

CHAPTER TWO
The Results of Privatizing Social Security
15

CHAPTER THREE
Why the Bush Approach to Terrorism Worked
29

CHAPTER FOUR
The Media and 911 Commission Did Not Tell Us the Truth
45

CHAPTER FIVE
What Happened to the Weapons of Mass Destruction
57

CHAPTER SIX
Junk Science, Global Warming and Cap & Trade
67

CHAPTER SEVEN
From Five Rogue Nations To One
87

CHAPTER EIGHT
The Two Wars in Iraq
95

CHAPTER NINE
How We Beat Al-Qaida and Won the
Iraq War Despite the Media
99

PROLOGUE

**I don't care which side the
truth is on, liberal or conservative,
I just want the truth so I can
decide for myself.**

A purpose of this book is to explain how a liberal can turn conservative without losing his morals. It is a wonderful place to be.

In the late 1960's, we liberals labeled all that our parents had built, including corporate America and the military, as "the establishment." We had seen the Watts riots in 1965 and then the Vietnam War, which seemed to represent senseless killing. We did not like what we saw. These events gave us a "cause" which was to reject everything, meaning the entire establishment. This left us with only a basic set of morals or ideals. The media also took up our cause.

A friend and I drove to San Francisco to attend a war protest march and concert. The protest march was to begin at Haight and Ashbury Streets and end in Golden Gate Park where there would be a concert. In front of us in the march was a protester wearing purple sweat pants. Occasionally, he would drop the back of his sweat pants. On his left cheek was painted the "F" word and on his right cheek was "Reagan." My friend and I decided this was not a very cerebral approach to our cause so we left before arriving at the park.

In retrospect, the media did not progress much past their rejection of the establishment. They specified the cause merely by becoming anti-Republican and anti-big business, with the environment being a subset of anti-big business. This was fine with me. However, I remember at home in San Bernardino, California walking around the backyard thinking, "Our plants are not dying from acid rain." Later the story morphed into, "The buildings are melting from acid rain." I noticed I was often confused with what I was hearing and reading because media reports did not match with my observations.

When the second oil crisis hit in 1978, the same finger pointing started again and I threw my pencils in the air. I thought, "I am a college graduate, I can do a research project." So I started a file on the energy crisis. It took about a year and a half to figure out what caused the energy crisis, however what shocked me was the fact that the media was literally lying to us. The crisis had absolutely nothing to do with the oil companies or their profits. But that is explained in Chapter One.

So I started watching the media with a critical eye and

began files on subjects that the media seemed to be distorting. The media was opposing big business and Republicans right or wrong. As I learned the truth about each subject, I became less and less confused. Confusion is the natural state of believing a dishonest media.

I became conservative but brought all my liberal ideals with me (Caring for the poor and programs to help them, caring for the elderly, caring for blacks and their plight, the environment, civil rights). Early on, I was implacable because of these ideals. However I began a progression of learning when I decided, "I don't care which side the truth is on, liberal or conservative, I just want the truth so I can decide for myself."

We are led to believe by the media that conservatives don't have these ideals, but that is not true. I feel comfortable on the conservative side with these morals. Conservatives are simply pragmatic about whether the government programs are working and they understand far better how to solve the problems that we liberals care so much about.

Having arrived on the conservative side, I look around at my liberal friends and family and realize I love them and there is nothing wrong with them. Caring for the poor and their basic ideals are good. They simply are misinformed by a dishonest media that opposes Republicans and big-business right or wrong. The media has driven a wedge between us. When a conservative talks, the liberal, in his mind, tries to label him a fascist, a racist, somewhere to the right of Attila the Hun, Hitler, a Nazi or a homophobe. When a liberal talks, the conservative is thinking, true, false, false, false, false, false assumption, false, false conclusion based on a false assumption.

My files evolved into what I would call historical essays written for myself to track the truth and keep my head screwed on straight. Most essays reveal what the media has tried to cover up to promote their cause. We cannot solve our problems with missing information and false facts. The purpose of the following essays is to display the dishonesty of the media.

My conclusion is to blame the media that has not pro-gressed beyond the butt cheek level of ideals that I saw in San Francisco.

CHAPTER ONE

HOW THE MEDIA BECAME DISHONEST

Confusion is the natural state of believing a dishonest media.

On June 23, 2006, the Los Angeles Times and the New York Times disclosed classified details about President Bush's "Swift" program for tracking finances of al-Qaida operatives. The information leaked from the Senate Foreign Intelligence Committee. Both newspapers were contacted by the administration and were told not to release the information. An administration employee appeared on Sean Hannity's radio show to say that he repeatedly sent letters with reasons and called repeatedly to convince the editors, Bill Keller of the N.Y. Times and Dean Baquet of the L.A. Times, not to run their stories. Both editors defied the White House's efforts to stop them and ran their stories.

As one attorney calling in to a radio show explained, "This act meets the criteria of treason." How and when did the media become so corrupt as to do something like this? This is an interesting question. Many Americans understand that the media is liberal and biased, however in their desperation to blame Republicans, the media has become corrupt and dishonest.

History of the Problem.

I entered college in 1969 and was immediately swept up into the war protest movement. I marched in San Francisco, attended Jerry Reuben and Jane Fonda rallies, registered as a Democrat and eventually voted for George McGovern. Our values were: save the environment, end racism, promote civil rights, reduce poverty for those less fortunate and for the elderly.

After Watergate, there was a noticeable change in the media's approach that made me skeptical of their stories. It seemed to me that suddenly, all reporters and editors wanted to become "investigative journalists" like Woodward and Bernstein. Much of our movement's attitude had permeated the media. The war had ended and concern shifted to the environment. We began to read and see investigative journalist reports about large corporations polluting the environment. *60 Minutes* became the most popular news show on television. Investigative journalism changed the approach to news. All the news services were getting into the act. Editors would call journalists into their office and say, "Go get a story on that chemical company that is dumping chemicals in the river." With this new approach, the outcome of the story was presumed and predetermined. This is the primary characteristic contributing to media dishonesty.

Over the years, my entire career has been to provide products and services to industrial customers. I have been in a number of chemical factories and understand their operations. Chemical factories are not much more than a blending process where liquids are brought in by rail, blended and sold in barrels. The various liquids are pumped from rail cars into large polymer or stainless steel tanks inside the factory. The liquids are then batched (pumped and measured) into blending tanks and then into barrels ready for shipment. There is no waste. The amounts not used remain in the inventory tanks. Occasionally, a factory employee would comment on the media attacks about their industry by explaining that chemical companies do not dump chemicals, they sell them. Imagine an investigative journalist confronting an executive with the accusation that he is dumping chemicals in the river. I believe the executive would walk that journalist through the entire factory and explain their process.

Most journalists would go back to their editor and say "There is no story here." And the editor says, "Oh come on, if you can't handle this, I will get someone who can." In this way, the honest reporters are shuffled to other stories and the lead stories are given to reporters who are willing to cut and paste interviews to match the predetermined outcome. This was the critical reason and time that the media became dishonest. But the story goes on.

In 1975, the media blamed the entire oil crisis on our oil companies. Republicans blamed OPEC. When the second oil crisis hit in 1978, I became insatiably curious. I could not stand the finger pointing and confusion. I decided to conduct my own research. The Los Angeles Times was viciously blaming the oil companies. In all the articles that I clipped over the next year, there was enough supply data to assemble a crude understanding of who was exporting to us and how much.

Our own domestic production was published each week in the Los Angeles Times Sunday business section. This number was provided by the oil industry and hovered at 10 million barrels per day of domestic production. It took about a year to assemble all of the supply data and determine our imports to be roughly 7 million barrels per day. Demand was fluctuating around 17 million barrels, equaling maximum supply.

I learned by reading industry publications that our oil companies purchased from the exporting nations in layered contracts. For instance, if an oil company felt they would need 1 million barrels per day, they might purchase 500,000 barrels per day at $8.00 per barrel for 10 years; 300,000 barrels per day at $10.00 per barrel for 5 years; 100,000 barrels per day at $12.00 per barrel for two years; 50,000 barrels per day in one year contracts for $13.00 per barrel and the remaining fluctuating amount of roughly 50,000 barrels per day would be purchased on the spot market for a higher price. This spot price might range from $13.00 to $20.00 per barrel depending upon demand of the various oil companies. It was this spot market price that we saw in the newspaper every day.

The truth of what happened was this: In 1970, the price of oil was about $1.25 per barrel. Our demand was high and increasing. OPEC exporters were matching the demand, though they were nearing their export capacity.

In May 1970, a bulldozer broke a pipeline near the Persian Gulf and the spot market price of oil doubled until the pipeline was repaired. Muammar al-Qadhafi of Libya noticed this and called Armand Hammer of Occidental Petroleum for a meeting. Qadhafi imposed a tax that matched the spot market price increase and Occidental's cost doubled.

Armand Hammer emerged from that meeting saying, "The western world will never be the same again." The other OPEC members began imposing taxes. During the first oil crisis in 1975, OPEC members imposed an approximate average $6.00 tax taking oil to about $8.00 and in the second crisis in 1978, another tax of about $5.00 taking the price to about $13.00 per barrel.

It took about a year and a half of homework and research to determine all this.

I was angered that I had to work so hard to find the truth.

I lost all trust in the Los Angeles Times and other news organizations most of whom had a predetermined outcome for their stories that our oil companies were to blame. Not one news organization reported the truth about either energy crisis, not one.

This is a second characteristic necessary to understanding the new media. When it comes to a story that the media wants to predetermine, the media flies in a single flock. Notice how they interview each other for these stories. Media hosts would interview other media members such as correspondents and bureau chiefs who reflect the flock mentality. They never interviewed Armand Hammer.

Bernard Goldberg who quit CBS News to report on media bias, in his book *Arrogance,* explained this flock mentality by essentially saying that, television news people wake up in the morning and read the New York Times trying to decide which will be the lead story of the day. They call each other to pin down the choice. For example, when a newspaper reporter coined the term "Star Wars" for Ronald Reagan's SDI proposal, Dan Rather squawked Star Wars and the entire media began squawking Star Wars like a flock of parrots.

In 1978, a CBS Television news reporter stuck a microphone in a nine year old girls face and asked, "Aren't you afraid that your next president might start a nuclear war?" The media's attack on Ronald Reagan began and did not stop until 1990, two years after he left office.

By this time, I was keenly aware of the media's two tactics, to predetermine the outcome of certain stories and to fly in a single flock, "parroting" the story. But the media pounced on the opposite side of every one of Reagan's proposals and later they did the same to President Bush. This brings us to a third observation necessary to determining truth in today's world. The media had become activist anti-Republican and anti-big business. These are the two templates, as some conservatives call it, through which all news must pass before it reaches us.

Some very dramatic news events that did not fit through these templates have not reached us, even to this day. I call these, media black-outs. For example, President Clinton turned down extradition of Osama bin-Laden. That's a big story! *Bill Clinton has admitted this and yet, reporters will not report it.*[1]

Conservatives mischaracterize the media as anti-Reagan or anti-Bush, but it is more accurate to note that the media is anti-Republican. It does not matter which Republican is in office. When the Democrats are out of power, the media becomes irrationally activist in their opposition to anything Republicans propose or try to accomplish.

In order to take an opposing view of someone who is correct, the reporter will necessarily have to be wrong. And to argue the case, the reporter must introduce false testi-

[1] Newsmax recording played on the Sean Hannity radio show many times. See further details in Chapter 4.

mony. So, editors moved reporters who were willing to twist the truth about Republicans and "big business" to the front-page stories, the stories that needed to squeeze through the template. And please observe, the media gives prime time coverage to those willing to lie if it helps make their point. A reporter will follow an accurate portrayal of a situation by saying, "but some say..," and proceed to quote people who are not telling the truth.

Media Canards.

I call twisted stories and fabrications by the media, "media canards." Each media canard starts with a single false news story and spreads through the flock in about a day.

To detect what might be a media canard use these criteria: Is it anti-Republican, anti-big business or pro-environmental and is it spread by the flock? To fly alone, do your homework, crunch some numbers, look skeptically at the story, be curious. Most of all, think for yourself.

When I was a liberal, I was confused most of the time. As mentioned, confusion is the natural state which arises from believing a dishonest media. What the media was telling me did not fit with observations or with actual numbers. As I researched subjects and discovered the truth, I became less and less confused.

Liberals and media disdain numbers, but quantifying

situations is the only way to build a structure of truth. By quantifying problems, I proved my right brain wrong so many times that I concluded that right brain intelligence is no insulation from being wrong. In other words, we observe intelligence as quick wittedness, good memory and reading retention, but when we read misinformation, remember and spew media misinformation, we may seem intelligent but our conclusions are wrong.

Over the years, I changed from a liberal to a conservative, but brought with me every one of those traditional liberal values.

Liberals with those good values cannot solve problems by following the media flock, which merely opposes Republicans and big business, right or wrong. For instance, a favorite liberal value of mine, and most liberals, is to provide support for the poor.

Who Really Lowered Taxes for the Poor?

Only twice since "The Great Society" began have we lowered income taxes for the poor. Both reductions in the lowest tax bracket were by Republicans, Ronald Reagan (from 22% to 15%) and George W. Bush (from 15% to 10%). During that time, Democrats had control of Congress for 25 years and never bothered to propose tax cuts for the poor. And don't kid yourself, standard deductions only cover, on average, about the first $6,000 of income. The poor do pay taxes.

Since we cannot trust the media to view anything from a conservative's perspective, we must learn to think for ourselves. For-instance lets do the math on spending for the poor.

Liberals Don't Give the Money to the Poor.

William Simon, Secretary of the Treasury under President Ford pointed out in his 1978 book, *A Time for Truth,* the poor are receiving a small portion of the money that we pour into social spending. To update Mr. Simon's example, let's divide current annual social spending (not including Social Security) of about $700 billion by approximately 35 million poor (including children and college students). The number comes to $20,000 per family member. That is $80,000 per year for a family of four poor people. They receive about $20,000 per year.

The next eight chapters are some examples of issues that have been muted by the media that both liberals and conservatives can ponder.

America's only serious problem is a dishonest media that has driven a wedge between us such that we can no longer intelligently debate true facts and therefore solve the simplest of problems.

CHAPTER TWO

THE RESULTS OF PRIVATIZING SOCIAL SECURITY

**We only learn what we see and hear.
It is better to learn what we can't
see and can't hear.**

In quantifying the demographics of poverty, we find that roughly one fourth of chronically impoverished people are the elderly trying to live on Social Security.

A simple spreadsheet (See following pages, Exhibit 1 of 2) tracking Dow Jones averages proves that had we privatized Social Security, a person who earned $15,000 per year (Exhibit 1) at age 21 and retired this year with an annual income of $57,928 at age 65, would have retired with over $1,050,000 in their Social Security account. This includes all the downturns including the 2008-2009 downturn.

The declining balance at an annual return of 5% would then provide that retired person with a retirement income of $83,077 per year until the money ran out at age 85. With

$83,077 per year, retirees could pay for a $20,000[1] per year private medical policy thereby eliminating Medicare. The retiree would still have $63,000 per year to age 85. What does this retiree get now from Social Security? The answer is about $9,900 per year, $3,000 below the poverty level.

Exhibit 2 shows that a current middle-income retiree would be receiving approximately $110,769 per year in retirement income!

Please take the time to review the charts carefully. They are easy to understand. The two charts (Exhibits 1 & 2) represent two different examples of retirees with two different incomes. Each example has two sections, a time period during working years that accumulates the money and a time period of retirement when the money is spent.

Exhibit 1 shows a beginning income of $15,000 per year at age 21 in the left column. The right column shows the accumulating wealth of the invested proceeds by using the actual Dow Jones averages. Notice the working years end on the following page at age 65 when the person has accumulated $1,054,008. The second section of Exhibit 1 shows in the right column the annual retirement amount of $83,077 per year to age 85.

---

[1] This is an estimate and it is certainly debatable. It would be provided by any qualified insurer willing to provide major medical benefits to Social Security recipients. Even if this number is off by say, fifty percent, it has a minor impact on the point or the retirement amount.

These numbers are only disputable in minor increments.[2] The examples are very conservative since the life expectancy is to about age 80, not 85. The numbers are even more conservative in that they assume all of us are stupid enough (as some of us are occasionally) to leave our money invested during the downturns.

(SEE CHARTS FOLLOWING PAGE)

---

[2] For example, the Dow Jones Averages are rounded off to the nearest 50 and there were slight modifications to the tax rates in the early years. However, the charts are accurate enough to properly display the point to be made.

EXHIBIT 1

**Your annual retirement income had your lifetime earnings grown
from $15,000/yr. to $57,928/yr: $83,077.**

YEAR	AGE	TAXED INCOME	SOCIAL SECURITY TOTAL TAX	DOW JONES AVERAGE	COMPOUND BALANCE INVESTED
1964	21	$15,000	$1,860	760	$2,110
1965	22	$17,250	$2,139	880	$4,920
1966	23	$19,838	$2,460	980	$8,218
1967	24	$22,813	$2,829	830	$9,356
1968	25	$26,235	$3,253	910	$13,825
1969	26	$26,760	$3,318	940	$17,708
1970	27	$27,295	$3,385	800	$17,951
1971	28	$27,841	$3,452	850	$22,741
1972	29	$28,398	$3,521	910	$28,116
1973	30	$28,966	$3,592	1,050	$36,586
1974	31	$29,545	$3,664	820	$31,433
1975	32	$30,136	$3,737	660	$28,308
1976	33	$30,739	$3,812	930	$45,259
1977	34	$31,353	$3,888	1,000	$52,846
1978	35	$31,980	$3,966	830	$47,153
1979	36	$32,620	$4,045	820	$50,581
1980	37	$33,272	$4,126	850	$56,709
1981	38	$33,938	$4,208	950	$68,084
1982	39	$34,617	$4,292	1,000	$76,185
1983	40	$35,309	$4,378	1,250	$100,705
1984	41	$36,015	$4,466	1,200	$100,964
1985	42	$36,735	$4,555	1,550	$136,295
1986	43	$37,470	$4,646	1,900	$172,767

EXHIBIT 1

Your annual retirement income had your lifetime earnings grown from $15,000/yr. to $57,928/year: $83,077.

YEAR	AGE	TAXED INCOME	SOCIAL SECURITY TOTAL TAX	DOW JONES AVERAGE	COMPOUND BALANCE INVESTED
1987	44	$38,220	$4,739	1,950	$182,178
1988	45	$38,984	$4,834	2,150	$206,192
1989	46	$39,764	$4,931	2,750	$270,041
1990	47	$40,559	$5,029	2,650	$265,068
1991	48	$41,370	$5,130	3,168	$323,014
1992	49	$42,198	$5,232	3,300	$341,923
1993	50	$43,041	$5,337	3,750	$394,614
1994	51	$43,902	$5,444	3,850	$410,726
1995	52	$44,780	$5,553	5,100	$551,434
1996	53	$45,676	$5,664	6,450	$704,565
1997	54	$46,589	$5,777	7,900	$870,032
1998	55	$47,521	$5,893	9,150	$1,014,520
1999	56	$48,472	$6,010	11,500	$1,282,634
2000	57	$49,441	$6,131	10,800	$1,210,318
2001	58	$50,430	$6,253	10,000	$1,126,455
2002	59	$51,439	$6,378	8,350	$945,916
2003	60	$52,467	$6,506	10,450	$1,191,953
2004	61	$53,517	$6,636	10,800	$1,238,733
2005	62	$54,587	$6,769	10,700	$1,233,969
2006	63	$55,679	$6,904	12,450	$1,443,820
2007	64	$56,792	$7,042	12,451	$1,450,979
2008	65	$57,928	$7,183	9,000	$1,054,008

EXHIBIT 1

		UNDER THE CURRENT SYSTEM YOU GET:	VS.	HAD WE PRIVATIZED SOCIAL SECURITY YOU WOULD GET:	
		SOC. SEC. INCOME/YR		INVESTED PROCEEDS	TOTAL INCOME/YR
2009	66	$9,905		$1,054,008	$83,077
2010	67	$9,905		$1,019,478	$83,077
2011	68	$9,905		$983,221	$83,077
2012	69	$9,905		$945,151	$83,077
2013	70	$9,905		$905,178	$83,077
2014	71	$9,905		$863,206	$83,077
2015	72	$9,905		$819,136	$83,077
2016	73	$9,905		$772,862	$83,077
2017	74	$9,905		$724,274	$83,077
2018	75	$9,905		$673,257	$83,077
2019	76	$9,905		$619,689	$83,077
2020	77	$9,905		$563,443	$83,077
2021	78	$9,905		$504,384	$83,077
2022	79	$9,905		$442,373	$83,077
2023	80	$9,905		$377,260	$83,077
2024	81	$9,905		$308,893	$83,077
2025	82	$9,905		$237,106	$83,077
2026	83	$9,905		$161,731	$83,077
2027	84	$9,905		$82,587	$83,077
2028	85	$9,905		-$515	$83,077

NOTES:
1. Assumed compound growth rate during retirement is 0.05%
2. On the previous page, the earnings growth rate decreases to 2% after the first five years.
3. On the previous page, the Social Security tax is combined contributions of employer and employee.

EXHIBIT 2

Your annual retirement income had your lifetime earnings grown from $20,000/yr. to $77,238/yr.: $110,769.

YEAR	AGE	TAXED INCOME	SOCIAL SECURITY TOTAL TAX	DOW JONES AVERAGE	COMPOUND BALANCE INVESTED
1964	21	$20,000	$2,480	760	$2,813
1965	22	$23,000	$2,852	880	$6,560
1966	23	$26,450	$3,280	980	$10,958
1967	24	$30,418	$3,772	830	$12,475
1968	25	$34,980	$4,338	910	$18,433
1969	26	$35,680	$4,424	940	$23,611
1970	27	$36,393	$4,513	800	$23,935
1971	28	$37,121	$4,603	850	$30,321
1972	29	$37,864	$4,695	910	$37,488
1973	30	$38,621	$4,789	1,050	$48,782
1974	31	$39,393	$4,885	820	$41,911
1975	32	$40,181	$4,982	660	$37,743
1976	33	$40,985	$5,082	930	$60,345
1977	34	$41,804	$5,184	1,000	$70,461
1978	35	$42,641	$5,287	830	$62,871
1979	36	$43,493	$5,393	820	$67,442
1980	37	$44,363	$5,501	850	$75,612
1981	38	$45,251	$5,611	950	$90,778
1982	39	$46,156	$5,723	1,000	$101,581
1983	40	$47,079	$5,838	1,250	$134,273
1984	41	$48,020	$5,955	1,200	$134,618
1985	42	$48,981	$6,074	1,550	$181,727
1986	43	$49,960	$6,195	1,900	$230,356
1987	44	$50,959	$6,319	1,950	$242,903

EXHIBIT 2

Your annual retirement income had your lifetime earnings grown from $20,000/yr. to $77,238/yr.: <u>$110,769.</u>

YEAR	AGE	TAXED INCOME	SOCIAL SECURITY TOTAL TAX	DOW JONES AVERAGE	COMPOUND BALANCE INVESTED
1988	45	$51,979	$6,445	2,150	$274,923
1989	46	$53,018	$6,574	2,750	$360,055
1990	47	$54,079	$6,706	2,650	$353,424
1991	48	$55,160	$6,840	3,168	$430,685
1992	49	$56,263	$6,977	3,300	$455,897
1993	50	$57,389	$7,116	3,750	$526,152
1994	51	$58,536	$7,259	3,850	$547,635
1995	52	$59,707	$7,404	5,100	$735,246
1996	53	$60,901	$7,552	6,450	$939,420
1997	54	$62,119	$7,703	7,900	$1,160,042
1998	55	$63,362	$7,857	9,150	$1,352,693
1999	56	$64,629	$8,014	11,500	$1,710,178
2000	57	$65,921	$8,174	10,800	$1,613,757
2001	58	$67,240	$8,338	10,000	$1,501,940
2002	59	$68,585	$8,505	8,350	$1,261,221
2003	60	$69,956	$8,675	10,450	$1,589,270
2004	61	$71,356	$8,848	10,800	$1,651,644
2005	62	$72,783	$9,025	10,700	$1,645,293
2006	63	$74,238	$9,206	12,450	$1,925,094
2007	64	$75,723	$9,390	12,451	$1,934,639
2008	65	$77,238	$9,577	9,000	$1,405,345

EXHIBIT 2

UNDER THE CURRENT SYSTEM YOU GET:				HAD WE PRIVATIZED SOCIAL SECURITY YOU WOULD GET:	
		SOC. SEC. INCOME/YR	**VS.**	INVESTED PROCEEDS	TOTAL INCOME/YR
2009	66	$13,207		$1,405,345	$110,769
2010	67	$13,207		$1,359,304	$110,769
2011	68	$13,207		$1,310,962	$110,769
2012	69	$13,207		$1,260,202	$110,769
2013	70	$13,207		$1,206,904	$110,769
2014	71	$13,207		$1,150,942	$110,769
2015	72	$13,207		$1,092,181	$110,769
2016	73	$13,207		$1,030,482	$110,769
2017	74	$13,207		$965,699	$110,769
2018	75	$13,207		$897,676	$110,769
2019	76	$13,207		$826,252	$110,769
2020	77	$13,207		$751,257	$110,769
2021	78	$13,207		$672,512	$110,769
2022	79	$13,207		$589,830	$110,769
2023	80	$13,207		$503,014	$110,769
2024	81	$13,207		$411,857	$110,769
2025	82	$13,207		$316,142	$110,769
2026	83	$13,207		$215,641	$110,769
2027	84	$13,207		$110,116	$110,769
2028	85	$13,207		-$686	$110,769

NOTES:
1. Assumed compound growth rate during retirement is 0.05%
2. On the previous page, the earnings growth rate decreases to 2% after the first five years.
3. On the previous page, the Social Security tax is combined contributions of employer and employee.

A proper application of privatization would require that all 401K's and IRA accounts be merged into the individual's Social Security account and the Social Security account would be self managed just like 401K's. Rules are already in place for the proper management of these funds. There would be no noticeable difference to the worker, except that his Social Security contribution begins accumulating in his own private account. There is no impact to the employer, because the company continues to make the same contribution to the worker's Social Security account. The worker's 401K simply merges and the worker has a private Social Security account.

The existing notion that the Social Security account is not touchable until retirement is a good one. This prevents us from withdrawing our retirement with a penalty. The government determined retirement age (62 and 65) could start getting younger instead of older since the amount of retirement funds would accumulate at such a high rate.

As mentioned, the accumulated funds would be more than enough to also privatize and eliminate Medicare. The retiree would have plenty of money to pay for his own private insurance. The government could easily make it a requirement that he do so, by requiring the fund administrator to disperse the premiums directly to the chosen insurance company.

The minor tax advantage of the 401K is dwarfed by the

staggering new investment returns in Social Security. For the employers this is generally a push. For workers it is a life changing advantage.

The affect on the economy would be positive since about $160 billion[3] per year in Social Security excess tax payments (the amount Congress keeps and does not pay to retirees) would be invested in the private sector instead of the government.

A close look at the exhibits reveals it is not true that during the downturns we will lose our money. Notice that the accumulating investment grows back after the downturns.

This brings us to the real reason privatization of Social Security is such a good idea. Let's compare the "rising ups and downs" of a privatized account versus a Social Security account. When you pay into your Social Security account, the principal balance goes "Poof" and it is gone. That's right, what you invest is given to others and any excess not paid to others is spent by Congress. Your Social Security principal balance drops to zero every year. Think about it this way. Imagine you have two different mutual funds. The first is called LF (Legitimate Fund). In the first year you invest $1,000. During the next year, the market goes down

---

[3] An estimated amount which varies from year to year.

20% so you have $800 and in the second year you invest another $1,000 so you now have $1,800. Simultaneously you invested in your other fund, SSF (Social Security Fund). Your first year $1,000 goes poof and then your second year $1,000 goes poof and you have a zero balance. So even though the market crashed 20%, you are far better off having invested in the Legitimate Fund.

It does not matter that the market goes up and down. What matters is that your principal is invested and it is yours. The government can't take it as they are doing now. Beside that, the invested funds do grow over time.

The media who tells us that "We can't privatize because the retirees will lose all their money," is on the opposite side of the truth. We lose our money when we put it in Social Security. The media will say, "But the government will pay you and they really care." Take a look at the exhibits again. They show a side by side comparison of the actual private returns and what Social Security actually pays us. The exhibits prove them wrong.

In May 1980, the Chilean government privatized their retirement system when Milton Friedman first proposed it. It worked similar to what the numbers suggest it would. José Piñera, the then Minister of Labor states,

"Chile's private pension system has been the main factor in increasing the savings rate to the level of an Asian tiger. Our rate is 26 percent of GNP, compared to about 15 per-

cent in Latin America... Pension reform has contributed strongly to an increase in the rate of economic growth. Before the 1970s Chile had a real growth rate of 3.5 percent. For the last 10 years we have been growing at the rate of 7 percent, double our historic rate. That is the most powerful means of eliminating poverty because growth increases employment and wages. Several experts have attributed the doubling of the growth rate to the private pension system." [4]

So Señior Piñera observed that the entire economy benefited due to the large increase in savings rate. A high savings rate in the private sector is beneficial because it increases capital investment which creates products and jobs.

The Chileans began by offering a choice to workers of the new privatized retirement system or the existing government system which was similar to our Social Security. Roughly half of the workers did not trust the private sector and opted for the government run system. Within the first two years many of them scrambled to get into the privatized system. Señior Piñera further states,

"Ninety percent of Chile's workers chose to move into the new system. We have calculated that the typical Chilean worker's main asset is not his small house or his used car

---

[4] CATO Policy Reports, *The Success of Chile's Privatized Social Security*, by José Piñera, former Minister of Labor and Current President of the International Center for Pension Reform.

but the capital in his pension account." [5] Investors Business Daily reports that, "The Chilean poverty rate dropped from 45% to 15% and per capita annual income is up from $1,400 in 1986 to $15,000 by 2009."

Every American, particularly young ones, should review these exhibits or any similar analysis. Why won't they? The media won't publish such proof because it supports a Republican idea. If a Democrat came up with the same plan, the media would praise it and promote it.

Think about what the media pounded into our heads when President Bush proposed that we at least partially privatize Social Security, "We can't because they will lose all their money." The exhibits certainly prove this wrong. And remember what the media said when President Reagan proposed to privatize Social Security, "Reagan is just trying to line the pockets of his rich friends." Do you see how the media has become shallow? Social Security is such a simple and easily solvable economic problem but we can't solve it because the media mindlessly opposes Republican ideas. Democrats believe what the media tells them so we can't agree.

Meanwhile many of our elderly, having invested enough of their hard earned dollars into the Social Security system to be millionaires, live in poverty.

---

[5] Ibid.

CHAPTER THREE

WHY THE BUSH APPROACH TO TERRORISM WORKED

Becoming liberal is an epiphany, becoming conservative is a learning process.

Ronald Kessler's new book, *The Terrorist Watch,* explains in detail the Bush approach to fighting terror. It is a must read for any American.

President Bush's approach to fighting terror has prevented over a hundred terrorist attacks and saved countless lives. It is shocking that the American media refuses to disclose this information when it is probably one of our country's greatest accomplishments and is so vital to our security.

A before and after comparison of our security agencies effectiveness helps tell the story.

Before Bush: The Clinton Administration

Six weeks after President Clinton first took office, Osama bin-Laden directed the placement of a truck bomb at a support column at the World Trade Center in an attempt to bring down the tower, which would have killed thousands of office workers. Few were killed and the attempt essentially failed. Four months later the CIA, with assistance from foreign law enforcement agencies, successfully traced the attack to Bin-Laden.

FBI agents requested an indictment naming Osama bin-Laden as a co-conspirator in the bombing of the World Trade Center. The FBI indictment was not executed until five years later in 1996. Meanwhile, Osama bin-Laden gained confidence that the U.S. would not retaliate.

By 1993, Bin-Laden had not only bombed the World Trade Center, he also bombed the Aden Hotel in Yemen in an attempt to kill 100 U.S. Air Force and Marine Officers who were commanding a squadron of transports to fly aid to Somalia.

Bin-Laden then financed and orchestrated the attack on our troops, who were delivering aid to Mogadishu, and bombed the U.S. military training facilities in Riyadh, Saudi Arabia. *At that point, the Saudis offered to arrest and extradite Bin-Laden, if they catch him in Saudi Arabia. President Clinton ignored the offer.*[1]

---

[1] Richard Miniter on Sean Hannity talk radio show, September 2, 2003.

In Sudan, he tried to recruit members of Hezbollah of Iran, Islamic Jihad of Egypt and Palestinian Hamas who had gathered for an annual meeting.

One of Sudan's ministers who sponsored the event, Hassan Turabi, later told Clinton's envoy Mansoor Ijaz, "Bin-Laden scared us. All he wanted was to talk Jihad (war) against the United States. No one joined his organization."

The other organizations were focused on their underground war with Israel, none of them wanted to fight the U.S. Turabi reported to the President of Sudan, Omar Hassan al-Bashir who also met with Bin-Laden. President al-Bashir also concluded that he did not want Bin-Laden in his country.

Al-Bashir later sent two offers to arrest and extradite Bin-Laden to President Clinton. The first offer was ignored and after the second offer was hand carried by an aide in March 1996, Clinton finally responded with a facsimile, "No, let him go, anywhere but Somalia." [2]

A week later, Bin-Laden left for Afghanistan with five members of al-Qaida. In Afghanistan, Osama bin-Laden built a number of training camps to train al-Qaida recruits. Over the next five years, it has been estimated that Bin-Laden recruited and trained approximately 10,000 al-Qaida

---

[2] Richard Miniter, *Losing bin-Laden*, Regency Publishing, Pg. 123: "Anywhere but Somolia." Also according to Mansoor Ijaz, who met with the president of Sudan, Omar al-Bashir, who handed Ijaz the facsimile which Ijaz told Hannity read, "No, let him go, anywhere but Somolia."

fighters.

Bin-Laden attacked us three more times with essentially no response from President Clinton. He blew up our embassy in Kenya, our embassy in Dar es-Salaam, Tanzania and the USS Cole in Yemen.

As was the tradition, President Clinton heard a weekly brief by the director of the CIA, James Woolsey. For what ever reason, Clinton did not want anything to do with Osama bin-Laden and discontinued the weekly CIA briefs in July, 1991, six months after he took office.[3]

This was after President Clinton knew Bin-Laden was responsible for bombing the Aden Hotel and the World Trade Center.

Later, a light aircraft accidentally crashed into the Whitehouse lawn. According to Kessler, James Woolsey would later joke, "That was Woolsey trying to get an appointment with the President." Woolsey further stated, "I didn't have bad relations with Clinton, I just didn't have any relations with him."

Clinton Builds The Wall.

The Foreign Intelligence Surveillance Act (FISA) bloomed from a distrust of the CIA in 1978. We have heard of "The Wall" (a tightening of the FISA law in 1995), which

---

[3] Ronald Kessler, *The Terrorist Watch,* Crown Forum Publisher, 2007: Page 87.

prevented the exchange of information between the CIA and FBI.

The Wall, "had essentially paralyzed the nation's effort to hunt down terrorists before they kill people," according to Kessler. The noted example of this was that the extensive history of violence and murder by Mohammed Atta provided by Israeli and CIA intelligence was blocked and not transferred to the FBI when Atta entered our country to fly an airliner into the World Trade Center. *The FBI didn't even know Atta was here.*

FISA established that local FBI investigations could not be supplemented with information gathered from the CIA except under certain circumstances. The FISA court required that information gathered from CIA intelligence sources had to be kept separate from information gathered by the FBI, which was developed for a criminal investigation.

As a result, CIA and FBI files could not be commingled. Each bit of CIA intelligence had to be identified as having been gathered by the CIA. This made CIA intelligence information difficult but not impossible to use in FBI prosecution cases.

In 1995, Richard Scruggs, chief counsel of the Justice Department Office of Intelligence Policy and Review wrote a memo which made an issue of contact between individuals as well as information stating, *"The simple legal response to parallel investigations is a 'Chinese Wall,' which divides the attorneys as well as the investigators."* [4]

This meant that not only were CIA and FBI files to be kept separate, the agents were not to communicate. The consequence was that the CIA evidence would not be admissible in court.

Deputy Attorney General Jamie Gorelick approved the memo and enforced Scruggs' dictum with a warning that FBI agents could be fired if they overstepped the boundaries. The threat worked and communication between the agencies ended.

President Clinton appointed Louis Freeh as FBI Director. Kessler states, *"Freeh's concept of investigations was limited to what he had done as an agent ten years earlier, knocking on doors and interviewing people. He did not understand how essential technology had become to law enforcement."*

Weldon Kennedy, associate deputy director for administration told Kessler that Freeh had a computer behind his desk but *"I never saw him use it, nor did I ever see it turned on."* Freeh was a field agent at heart and proceeded to expand the number of field offices, but did not allocate money to communications and technology. The FBI was not capable of collecting or processing information about numerous terrorists from the CIA.

---

[4] Ibid. *The Terrorist Watch*, Page 20.

The FBI was a low technology agency that reacted to crimes after they occurred and then proceeded with an investigation and prosecution.

The CIA was a good information gathering organization with no presidential authority to report to, limited ways to prosecute through the FBI, and not much cooperation in or out of the country.

After Clinton: The Bush Administration

President Bush inherited a CIA that was numbed by inaction from the previous administration. The good work by agents was wasted or ignored and the agency had devolved to people justifying the absence of retaliation by labeling each opportunity to attack Bin-Laden as "un-actionable."

Nevertheless, President Bush liked the existing CIA Director, George Tenet, and continued him as director.

Kessler claims, *"Both men were focused, prized action over words....and like Bush, Tenet could be blunt."*

Bush fired Louis Freeh, and on July 5, 2001 appointed Robert Mueller Director of the FBI.

Mueller reported that he and Tenet met daily with the President. "The President seemed to appreciate the intelligence reports, but the President would say, '*I want to know what you have to say about the terrorist threats that haven't materialized yet and how are we going to prevent them?*'"

But Mueller reported back that the FBI was not designed

that way, it was structured as an arrest and prosecution agency. Also, the FBI was a lumbering bureaucracy, layered with Justice Department and FISA attorneys.

Kessler said, "....*Mueller had met with Bob Dies, the FBI's computer guru. Mueller listed standard software such as Microsoft Office that he wanted on his computer. Dies told him none of it would work with anything else in the bureau. Mueller was flabbergasted...The FBI's computers, which were 386s, were so primitive no one would take them, even as a donation....They were pre-Pentium machines incapable of using current software or even working with a mouse.*" In addition, the FBI system could not email outside the agency.

In the weeks following 9/11, the press essentially blamed the United States, and searched for a reason that we were attacked.

Was our base in Saudi Arabia the reason Bin-Laden attacked us? What had we done? They also blamed the CIA and FBI. President Bush took a different approach and visited both agencies to speak with the staffs.

George Tenet recalled, "*He said, 'I trust you and I need you.' He could have cut us off at our knees. Instead, he said, 'I have enormous confidence in the men and women of this organization. I know what your work has been like.'*"

Tenet said, "*If you don't think that made a difference in everything that has happened since, you don't understand the relationship between the CIA and the President. Our boss was at our back. There isn't enough money in the world to replace what that meant."*

President Bush recognized the problems that the agencies were having and began work on the Patriot Act to break the deadlock of communication between the agencies and lay a legal groundwork for a new approach to fighting terror.

Bush and Donald Rumsfeld devised a remarkably different approach to fighting terror. They decided that reacting to terror was the wrong approach, instead they must prevent it.

Rather than lob a cruise missile at a single target, they decided to treat terror as an international crime problem. Therefore, they would need to capture the terrorists in their home countries before the crimes were planned and executed.

To do this, would mean they must solicit the cooperation of the nations where terrorists operate. The President outlined this strategy in his address to the nation on September 20th. Paraphrasing and quoting:

We must fight this enemy in three ways, 1) Terrorists must be fought in their own land. "...the only way to defeat terrorism as a threat to our way of life is to stop it, eliminate it, and destroy it where it grows." 2) Therefore, we must have the cooperation of the leadership in the countries where terrorists operate.

President Bush called upon all nations to help by saying, *"Either you are with us, or you are with the terrorists."* Nearly all nations agreed to help. 3) *"We will starve terrorists of funding."*

He asked other nations for *"help of police forces, intelligence services, and banking systems around the world."* Later, Bush and Rumsfeld added a fourth strategy of tracking terrorist communications.

Bush Breaks Down The Wall.

The Patriot Act, not only broke down "The Wall" between the CIA and the FBI, but it allowed banks to assist in the shut down of funding to terrorist organizations.

President Bush encountered seemingly insurmountable problems that conflicted with his vision to fight terror worldwide. The FBI was a domestic agency gone to waste in international jurisdictions. Yet it was an agency with the skills to track and capture covert operators such as the Mafia, (or al-Qaida).

So President Bush transformed the FBI into an international agency, like the CIA. If an agent was dogging a local terrorist, he did not need the CIA to go overseas for him to follow the money or leads to other terrorists. Under President Bush the new approach was prevention of the crime, not reaction to the crime. The agents were told, don't arrest them yet, use them to find other terrorists and track them all over the globe...discover the plan of the terrorist cell and prevent the act before it happens, but collect all the conspirators at once if possible. Tracking terrorists became like a Mafia sting operation.

Terrorists were to be held as enemy combatants so evidence gathered by both agencies could be used against them in a military court and so they could be returned to custody of a cooperating nation.

The President further recognized there was no synergy between the agencies and the agents could stumble over each other or work on the same terror cell thereby wasting effort. He formed an umbrella agency, which he named the National Counterterrorism Center (NCTC). He named Vice Admiral John Scott Redd as Director.

The President requested standardized reporting software and a secure information website so both CIA and FBI agents could post files on each terrorist cell they were tracking. Each agent was given a secure access code and entered terrorists names, bio, locations, aliases, cell activities, everything they new about the suspected terrorist and his cell.

The underlying "hard-drive" for the website is what Vice Admiral Redd calls, *"The mother of all databases,"* the Terrorist Information Datamart Environment (TIDE).[5]

Whether it comes in from an operations cable, from agents, the CIA, NSA, FBI or foreign intelligence, it goes

---

[5] Ibid. *Terrorist Watch*, Page 166.

into that database.

Each electronic file on an individual terrorist includes hyperlinks to the originating information, including FBI files, fingerprints and photographs. Iris scans, DNA data and facial recognition software were added later.

The TIDE data also is sent to the FBI and posted on their screening center website where customs officials and police officers throughout the nation can check during traffic stops or any routine interrogation.

The information began to flood in to the NCTC from our agents and agencies. FBI and CIA agents, who had previously been restricted from communicating, were sharing information freely from their respective stations, and doing so instantaneously. The speed of communication took a leap forward, which was critical to preventing terrorist acts before they happened.

Then the President made a stunning request. He insisted that the NCTC website and database be made available to other nations. To do this, they created a separate classified website so truly domestic intelligence could be kept separate at the NCTC. They called the new website NCTC On-Line.

So far, five thousand agents and analysts throughout the world have been given security clearance to enter the website. They can search for "Hezbollah" or "Mamdouh Salim" and link to related data. Postings can be made for new data and there are secure chat rooms.

Vice Admiral Redd claims, *"Anybody with the right clearance can get on there and say, 'What do you make of this?'...Nothing like this existed prior to 9/11."*

The NCTC On-Line exploded with names and aliases of suspected terrorists providing a worldwide intelligence spider web for terrorists. Pakistani secret service agents can quickly identify names with al-Qaida links. Agents in Yemen become as knowledgeable as our CIA about suspects.

Today, al-Qaida operatives can hardly travel without being tracked. Al-Qaida can only communicate by courier. The results are obvious.

Since 9/11, all eighteen attempted terrorist attacks on the United States have been prevented, (see below). But even more remarkable, is the fact that over 100 terrorist attacks have been prevented in other parts of the world.

Rather than malign the president with media canards such as "he had no plan" and "his failed policies," we should thank President Bush for what is clearly a remarkable accomplishment.

List of attempted terrorist attacks upon the United States since 9/11:
1. Abu Zubaydah – The Library Tower in Los Angeles, among other buildings. Incarcerated in – Guantanamo Bay, Cuba.

2. Abdullah al-Muhajir - Attempted bombing of an apartment building in Chicago. Incarcerated in – High Security Supermax ADX, Florence, Colorado.

3. Binyam Muhammad – Attempted bombing of a highly populated mall in Chicago with "weapons combining conventional explosives with radio-active material to be dispersed over a wide area." Incarcerated in – Guantanamo Bay, Cuba.

4. Ramsey Yousef – (Manila). Planned to "blow up as many as a dozen commercial airliners crossing the Pacific" from Manila to the United States. Incarcerated in – Guantanamo Bay, Cuba.

5-9. Khalid Sheikh Mohammed – (And numerous conspiring terrorists) Caught with plans on laptops to blow up the following:
  -American Consulate in Karachi, Pakistan.
  -A U.S. nuclear power plant.
  -The Sears Tower in Chicago.
  -New York Stock Exchange.
  -Empire State Building.
  -Brooklyn Bridge and another suspension bridge in New York.
  Incarcerated in – Guantanamo Bay, Cuba.

10. Riduan Hambali - (Indonesia). Caught with preparations and plans to hijack, crash and detonate an airliner bound from Indonesia to the U.S. Leader of the Islami

yah/al-Qaida cell responsible for the Bali nightclub bombing which killed 202 people. Incarcerated in – Guantanamo Bay, Cuba.

11. Majid Kahn – Plotted to blow up a "major petroleum infrastructure," in the United States. Incarcerated in – Guantanamo Bay, Cuba.

12. Talib Abu Salam Ibn Shareef – Attempted to place a bomb in a trash can at a Mall on the Friday before Christmas in Rockford, Illinois. Charged with "attempting to destroy a building with fire or explosion and one count of attempting to use a Weapon of Mass Destruction." Incarcerated in – Maryland, USA.

13-15. Fifteen Hijackers – (London). Attempted to hijack three British Air fights at Heathrow Airport nearly simultaneously as follows:
-British Air flight bound for New York.
-British Air flight bound for Washington, D.C.
-British Air flight bound for Los Angeles with a target of Las Vegas.
Plot was "intended by our enemies to be a second 9/11." Incarcerated in – England.

16. Mohamad Shnewer, Argon Abdullahhu, Eljvir Duka, Dritan Duka, Shain Duka and Serdar Tatar. – The conspirators were from an al-Qaida cell in Bosnia (former Yugoslavia). The Duka brothers were Albanian Moslems from Bosnia. They were, "Radical Islamists

trained as long range rifle experts" experienced at sniping Serb police as they patrolled at night. They intended to "kill as many soldiers as possible" at Fort Dix Army Post in New Jersey.

Incarcerated in – Camden, New Jersey.

17. Hassem Hammoud – (Beirut). Plot to blow up the PATH train tunnels under the Hudson River between New York and New Jersey. Incarcerated in – Lebanon.

18. Hamid Hayat – Plotted various attacks on a supermarkets and hospitals in the United States. Incarcerated in – Lodi, California.

CHAPTER FOUR

THE MEDIA AND 9/11 COMMISSION DID NOT TELL US THE TRUTH

The future is like wine. We don't know what to expect until we've tasted it, but then it's too late to improve it.
-Modified from *Excaliber*

On August 11th, 2005, Michael Savage (talk radio host) reported that Mohammed Atta had been tracked to the United States by military intelligence. The military tried to transfer the matter to the FBI, along with Atta's criminal history and his terrorist activities.

Acting on the 1995 directive by President Clinton's Justice Department Council, Jaime Gorelick, two department of defense attorneys blocked this transfer of information.

Mohammed Atta subsequently flew an airliner into the World Trade Center on September 11, 2001.

Here is a little history as Richard Miniter, author of *Losing Bin-Laden*, talk radio and a few journalists have pieced together:

December 1992, one month after President Clinton is elected, Osama bin-Laden declares war (jihad) on the United States. A videocassette of this threat is delivered to Al-Jazeera and, later in 1993, it was delivered to the Clinton Administration.

December 29, 1992 Osama bin-Laden bombs the Aden Hotel in Yemen in an attempt to kill 100 U.S. Air Force and Marine officers who had gathered to consult, and celebrate the New Year. The officers were commanding the transport Squadron 352 that were to fly KC130 Hercules transports with aid to Somalia. Yemen police find instructions from bin-Laden in the bombers hotel room and notify Interpol to seek and arrest Osama bin-Laden.

February 26, 1993 Osama bin-Laden bombs the World Trade Center in New York City. The bomb was placed in a truck at a support column in the parking structure. Clearly the intent was to cause a collapse of the tower. Within several months the CIA tracked the attack to Ramsey Yousef and Osama bin-Laden.

Approximately June and again in July 1993 Bin-Laden finances and calls for attacks on U.S. troops delivering aid in Mogadishu.

August 31, 1993 Mohammed Atta and fifty Hamas criminals are released from prison in Israel. The Israeli's had agreed to release most Hamas prisoners to accommodate

the Oslo Agreement negotiated by Warren Christopher and
Bill Clinton. Yasser Arafat insisted that all prisoners must
be released. The Israelis had refused to release these fifty
prisoners because they were known to have murdered innocent Israelis, but Clinton agreed with Arafat and insisted that
all prisoners be released. Atta had been convicted of blowing up a bus full of Israeli citizens in 1986. Israeli intelligence tracks Atta and informs U.S. military intelligence of
his whereabouts and history.

Late 1993, Osama bin-Laden claims credit for the attack
on the World Trade Center and renews his threats to the
United States in another tape sent to Al-Jazeera.

June 1995, Rush Limbaugh criticizes Jaime Gorelick's
directive to block the flow of communication between the
CIA, Defense Department and the FBI.

In 1978, Democrats had authored legislation (FISA) to
limit powers of the CIA and written communication to the
FBI, but never to block communication of a national security matter or communication about known dangerous persons.

Gorelick's directive created a "Chinese Wall....of communication" between agents of the CIA and the FBI. It included a threat that FBI agents could be fired for not com-
plying. Apparently the threat worked because communication between the agencies stopped.

November 13, 1995, Osama bin-Laden bombs U.S.

military training facilities in Riyadh, Saudi Arabia.

February 1996, Sudan's foreign minister Ali Taha offers to the U.S. Sudan Ambassador Timothy Carney that Sudan arrest and extradite Osama bin-Laden. The foreign minister's hope was to normalize relations with the U.S. There was no response.

March 1996, Sudan's President Omar Hassan al-Bashir sends General Elfatih Erwa to the United States with an offer to arrest and extradite Osama bin-Laden to the United States.

Rather than accept the extradition, Bill Clinton tried unsuccessfully to convince the Saudi government to take him. That effort failed. U.N. ambassador Madeline Albright reasoned, "We did not have a civil case against Bin-Laden." Bill Clinton ultimately told Sandy Berger to turn down the offer. President Clinton would later respond with the same reason, that "we did not have a civil case against him" in response to a reporter who asked him why he refused extradition of Bin-Laden.

This reasoning was clearly flawed since the F.B.I. had requested indictment of Osama bin-Laden as a co-conspirator for the bombing of the World Trade Center.

The extradition offer is made *again* a few weeks later since Bin-Laden was aware that he had been asked to leave Sudan and was preparing to leave. Finally, Ambassador Carney delivered the Clinton administration's final decision via facsimile: *"No. Let him go, anywhere but Somalia."* [1]

On May 10, 1996 Bin-Laden relocates to Afghanistan. Bin-Laden allies with the Taliban and begins plans for further attacks, including a second attack on the World Trade Center.

In fall of 1996, bin-Laden builds the first of several al-Qaida training camps. It has been estimated that Bin-Laden trained ten thousand al-Qaida fighters at these camps in the ensuing five years.

President Clinton's own emissary to Sudan, Mansoor Ijaz, would later recount that Osama bin-Laden had been in Sudan to meet with Egypt's Islamic Jihad, Iran's Hezbollah and Palestinian Hamas. Sudanese intelligence had collected photocopies of passports, affiliations with the aforementioned groups and numerous other details, all of which, Ijaz had made known to Sandy Berger and Susan Rice of the State Department.

In February 1996, to normalize relations with the U.S., Al-Bashir asked Ijaz to offer this intelligence data to President Clinton.

Ijaz inspected the intelligence data and recognized the significance of home addresses, I.D.'s, photos of over 500 terrorists. He took the offer to Sandy Berger and Susan Rice of the State Department. No action was taken.

---

[1] Richard Miniter. *Losing bin-Laden*, Regency Publishing, Page 123. Also see footnote on page 31 herein.

In Ijaz's own words, *"U.S. authorities repeatedly turned intelligence data away, first in February 1996; then again in August when, at my suggestion Sudan's Hassan Turabi wrote directly to Clinton; then again in April 1997, when I persuaded Bashir to invite the FBI to come to Sudan and view the data; and finally in February 1998, when Sudan's intelligence chief, Gutbi al-Mahdi, wrote. The silence of the Clinton Administration in responding to these offers was deafening."*

Mansoor Ijaz further stated, *"Bin-Laden left for Afghanistan, taking with him Ayman Zawahiri, considered by the U.S. to be the planner of the September 11 attacks; Mamdouh Mahmud Salim (al-Qaida technical expert who traveled frequently to Germany to acquire electronic equipment); Wadih El- Hage who planned the U.S. Embassy bombings in Tanzania and Kenya; Fazul Abdullah Mohammed and Saif Adel who are accused of carrying out the embassy attacks"....The two men who piloted the planes into the twin towers, Mohamed Atta and Marwan Al-Shehhi, prayed at the same Hamburg mosque as did Salim."* [2]

August 7, 1998 Bin-Laden bombs the embassies in Nairobi, Kenya and Dar es Salaam, Tanzania.

October 12, 2000 Bin-Laden attacks the USS Cole.

---

[2] Mansoor Ijaz, "Clinton Let Bin Laden Slip Away and Metastasize," December 5, 2001. Also, Mansoor Ijaz, "The Clinton Intel Record," National Review Online, April 28, 2003.

September 11, 2001 Mohammed Atta, under the direction of Osama bin-Laden and Ayman Zawahiri, flies an airliner into the World Trade Center.

September 2, 2003 Richard Miniter (Wall Street Journal reporter in Europe) appears on the Sean Hannity radio show to discuss his new book, *Losing Bin-Laden*, and reveals that President Clinton had turned down multiple offers to extradite Osama bin-Laden.

Hannity and a furious call-in audience were stunned. Miniter appeared eight more times that month on FOX News Channel Television shows hosted by Fox & Friends, Shepard Smith, Brit Hume, Geraldo Rivera, Tony Snow, Greta Van Susteren, Fox News Live and ending on September 25 with Bill O'Reilly.

Two liberal news stations, CNN and MSNBC, met with Miniter using edited clips rather than interviews and cut to commentators who literally called him a liar. While Miniter made the Fox News circuit, Hannity interviewed on his radio show persons mentioned in Miniter's book in an effort to corroborate his story.

October 2003, Democrats, at the urging of Jay Rockefeller (Democrat, West Virginia) organize the 9/11 commission "to investigate what went wrong."

Notice this occurred two years after 9/11! Why would the Democrats rush to put together a commission two years after the disaster? The revealing fact is that the 9/11 commission was launched just two weeks after Richard Miniter and Sean Hannity broke the story that President Clinton had refused extradition of Bin-Laden. It is also telling that the 9/11 commission chose to investigate a scope of time that started after the extradition offers.

Days before Sandy Berger was to testify, an unnamed Republican in the defense department called Rush Limbaugh to say that, "Sandy Berger has been stealing files and taking them home."

The only conceivable conclusion was that Sandy Berger was removing the extradition offer(s). Later, it is found that Sandy Berger shredded the files. Berger eventually pleaded guilty and was fined for removing the documents from the National Archives.[3]

None other than Jaime Gorelick is one of the commission members. Hannity and Limbaugh follow every detail of the commission's investigation.

In the first week, the commission members grilled members of President Bush's cabinet in hope of finding any fault. In the second week, one of the commission members complained to Colin Powell that there was not sufficient communication among our agencies.

Rush Limbaugh reacted with disgust. The next day Limbaugh played copies from his show in June of 1995 that

---

[3] Associated Press, "Inspector General Says Former National Security Adviser Sandy Burger Hid Classified Docs" December 21, 2006.

criticized Jaime Gorelick for writing the directive to stop communication from the military or CIA to the FBI. The commission's own member was at fault. The matter was dropped and the commission seemed to back off from accusing President Bush.

The Commission's scope conveniently began in 1998, two years after the last of the extradition offers, and ended well into the Bush Administration. Therefore the movie, "Path to 9/11," which disputed the Commissions report also missed the extradition offers.

As you may recall, the Commission succeeded in convincing the public that "Both administrations were at fault."

Now, as Michael Savage (talk radio) pointed out, it seems that such blocked communication was most definitely relevant. The arrival of Mohammed Atta and other members of his terrorist cell to the U.S. were reported by the military's intelligence unit "Able Danger" in 1999. Due to Jaime Gorelick's directive, tracking of Atta and his accomplices stopped at that point.

December 21, 2006 the Inspector General report concludes, *"President Clinton's national security advisor removed classified documents from the National Archives, hid them under a construction trailer and later tried to find the trash collector to retrieve them......Berger took the documents in the fall of 2003 while working to prepare himself and the Clinton Administration witnesses for testimony to* *the 9/11 commission....Berger pleaded guilty to unlawfully removing and retaining classified documents. He was fined fifty thousand dollars, ordered to perform 100 hours of community service and was barred from access to classified materials for three years... Berger had destroyed, cut into small pieces three of the four documents."*

Here is what we should have learned from a truthful media and 9/11 commission:

The mainstream media knew most of this all along and covered it up. A story about the extradition offer was on the newswires and the media, in their zeal to protect Democrats and harm Republicans, only harmed Americans by covering it up.

Proof of this is an article published by Washington Post staff writer, Barton Gellman on Wednesday, October 3, 2001, three weeks after destruction of the World Trade Center. The article starts by saying, "The government of Sudan, employing a back channel direct from its President to the Central Intelligence Agency, offered in early spring of 1996 to arrest Osama bin-Laden and place him in custody (U.S. or Saudi) according to officials and former officials of all three countries. The Clinton administration struggled to find a way to accept the offer in secret contacts that stretched from a meeting at a Rosslyn Hotel on March 3, to a fax that closed the door on the effort 10 weeks later."

This article was on the news wire so we know that the media knew about the extradition offers. There are no other articles to be found anywhere in the media about the extradition offer after this one publication.

It wasn't until the truth started to come out on the Sean Hannity show (six years after the incident and two years after 9/11) that Jay Rockefeller hurriedly put together the 9/11 commission to smother the information that Richard Miniter was providing to the public.

Irrefutable proof of the extradition offers exists because one honest reporter at News Max recorded a speech where Clinton admitted that he turned down extradition of Bin-Laden.

Apparently, mainstream media reporters asked Clinton to speak to them, presumably about what to do or say about the extradition offers. Clinton addressed a select group of media reporters.

A News Max reporter was so disgusted with what he heard that he eventually gave a recording of the speech to Sean Hannity. Hannity has played it many times on the air. It is telling that even after hearing the admission from Clinton, no other reporters that attended that select press conference said a word to the public.

So the concern is not only about the incompetence of President Clinton, et.al. The point to be made is that our liberal media is so dishonest that they will cover up what is the biggest story of our time in order to protect their favored Democrat President.

Had Jaime Gorelick not blocked communication from the CIA to the FBI, Mohammad Atta might have been prevented from destroying the World Trade Center.

Had Madeline Albright and/or Bill Clinton told Sandy Berger to accept extradition of Osama bin-Laden, 9/11 and the death of three thousand innocent Americans likely would have been prevented.

And as Mansoor Ijaz noted, al-Qaida consisted of six people at the time of the extradition offers and Bin-Laden trained approximately 10,000 Al-Qaida fighters afterward.

The disaster is that our corrupt and dishonest media covered up the incident of the extradition offers and we did not learn of it until seven years after it happened.

CHAPTER FIVE

WHAT HAPPENED TO THE WEAPONS OF MASS DESTRUCTION IN IRAQ

The media's power to deceive is nearly total.

The American media has been silent about what can only be described as overwhelming evidence that Saddam Hussein did have weapons of mass destruction (WMD) just prior to our invasion of Iraq. The evidence shows that Saddam shipped the WMD to Syria over several months until about January of 2003, when we began our invasion of Iraq.

Saddam's own Vice-Air Marshall, General Georges Sada first reported shipments of WMD to U.S. intelligence and the information was later declassified and detailed in his book, *Saddam's Secrets*. General Sada said, "..as a former general officer who not only saw these weapons but witnessed them being used on orders of the air force commanders and the president of the country...I know how and when they were transported and shipped out of Iraq." [1]

---

[1] Sada, George. *Saddam's Secrets*. Dallas: Integrity Publishers, 2006: 252

In 2002, the United Nations, having been rebuffed by Saddam for eleven years, finally added the threat of force to U.N. Resolution 1441 in the 15th and 16th amendments of that resolution. The title of the 15th amendment states:

SECURITY COUNCIL HOLDS IRAQ IN "MATERIAL BREACH" OF DISARMAMENT OBLIGATIONS.
OFFERS FINAL CHANCE TO COMPLY, UNANIMOUSLY ADOPTING RESOLUTION 1441. RECALLS REPEATED WARNING OF 'SERIOUS CONSEQUENCES' FOR CONTINUED VIOLATIONS [2]

The resolution, which Saddam had originally signed in 1991, stated that Iraq was to disclose all WMD and destroy them in the presence of U.N. inspectors.

Both the 15th and 16th amendments threatened the use of force and extended Iraq's compliance date to offer a "final opportunity to comply."

The Resolution summary states, "On November 8, 2002, the UN passed resolution 1441 urging Iraq to disarm or face 'serious consequences.' The resolution passed with a 15 to 0 vote, supported by Russia, China, France and Arab countries like Syria. This gave the resolution wider support than even the 1990 Gulf War Resolution." [3]

The amendments were passed unanimously and the French ambassador vetoed his own vote after we sortied our

---

[2] United Nations Press Release, SC/7564, August 11, 2002.
[3] United Nations Resolution 1441 Resolution Statement, for General Publication.

fleet.

Saddam had about a year of warning as he listened to the U.N. threats. General Sada points out, "Saddam realized, this time, the Americans are coming. They handed over the weapons of mass destruction to the Syrians." [4]

General Sada states the following in several pages of his book: "Saddam had ordered our weapons teams to hide the WMD in places no military commander or United Nations inspector would expect to find them. So they hid them in schools, private homes, banks, business offices, and on trucks that were kept constantly moving back and forth from one end of the country to the other. And then fate stepped in. On June 4, 2002, a three mile long irrigation dam….in Zeyzoun, Syria, collapsed, inundating small villages and destroying scores of homes…When Syrian President Bashar al -Assad asked for help from Jordan and Iraq, Saddam knew what he wanted to do.

For Saddam, the disaster in Syria was a gift, and there, posing as shipments of supplies and equipment to aid the relief effort, were Iraq's WMD.

Weapons and equipment were transferred both by land and by air…Instead of using military vehicles or aircraft which would have been apprehended and searched by coalition forces, Saddam's agents used civilian airlines….and eighteen-wheeler trucks.

---

[4] Ira Stoll, "Iraq's WMD Secreted in Syria, Sada Says", The New York Sun, January 26, 2006.

The plans for transferring these weapons were concocted by Ali and Ali. Our Ali was Ali Hussein al-Majid (Chemical Ali), and their Ali was General Abu Ali, who was a cousin of Syrian President Bashir al-Assad. For once in the long history of belligerence between Iraq and Syria, there was complete agreement between them.

They arranged for the operation to be conducted like a regular business deal and everything was paid for, up front and in cash. The tab for the fifty-six sorties (multiple truck convoys) of highly dangerous contraband was enormous, but for Saddam it was worth every penny...To keep these illegal transfers under wraps, the two Ali's worked through a false company called SES.

This company had played a key role in....transporting the illegal sale of oil, natural gas, gasoline, and other re-sources....defying United Nations sanctions." [5]

Larry Elder among other conservative talk radio hosts, were the few who interviewed General Sada. Elder, in an attempt to obtain corroboration interviewed terrorism expert John Loftus, a former Justice Department prosecutor, Army officer, and terrorism expert. Loftus once held some of U.S.'s highest security clearances.

Loftus was asked by Larry Elder, "It seems to me that this is a huge, huge story. Why has this not been reported in

---

[5] Sada, George. *Saddam's Secrets*. Dallas: Integrity Publishers, 2006: 258 -260

the press?" Loftus said, "It's embarrassing to them (the press). They've staked their reputations that this stuff was not there." [6]

Loftus also stated that Saddam's supply of WMD included Sarin and VX liquefied gasses.

U.N. inspectors, in 1996, had cataloged and photographed many tons of VX gas in Iraq. Subsequently, Saddam kicked out the inspectors.

General Sada claimed in his book that Saddam's engineers manufactured very large amounts of both gasses. And Loftus said, "VX gas is very rare and very difficult to manufacture and the large stockpiles had been known to be in Iraq."

So is General Sada a liar?

The American media might hope so, except the Israeli's have corroborated his story. Apparently, Israeli spy satellites observed multiple truck shipments over several months in late 2002 which went to three different bunkers in Syria.

Israel's Lt. General MosheYaalon said, "We very clearly saw that something crossed into Syria." [7]

Kenneth Timmerman, who is an investigative reporter for *Insight Magazine,* interviewed a senior U.S. administration official who said, "We have six or seven credible re-

---

[6] Elder, Larry. *Radio Interview with John Loftus.* May 6, 2004
[7] Statement to an Israeli newspaper, as reported by the *Post-Gazette* Toledo, Ohio Sunday May 2, 2004.

ports of Iraqi weapons being moved into Syria before the war."

Timmerman stated, "A Syrian intelligence officer, in letters smuggled to an anti-regime activist in Paris, identified three sites in Syria where Iraqi WMD are being stored. The three sites were the same as those identified earlier by a Syrian Journalist who defected to Europe." [8]

And on December 23, 2002 Israel's prime minister, Ariel Sharon, appeared on Israel's channel 2 to give some details. According to the *Middle East Quarterly* Sharon stated, "Chemical and biological weapons….have been moved from Iraq to Syria." [9]

Sharon did not state the location of the bunkers, only that the shipments contained WMD. So the story seems to have been common knowledge in the Middle East, but not reported in the western press.

General Sada surmised that the Bush administration and the Israelis have classified further information because they do not want attention drawn to the matter which may prompt Syria to disperse or relocate the WMD.

General Sada said, "I have discussed the subject with officials at the Pentagon, but until now the way these weapons were transported has been a military secret. …. It's not

---

[8] Timmerman's statements are assembled from Timmerman articles by the Post-Gazette, Toledo Ohio, May 2, 2004.
[9] Ira Stoll, "Iraq's WMD Secreted in Syria, Sada Says", The New York Sun, January 26, 2006.

something that has been widely discussed either in Iraq or in America, mainly because of what might happen if these matters were made public. ..Part of the concern, I believe, is because of where these weapons and materials were taken."[10]

Apparently this policy paid off because in April 2004, an Israeli spy satellite observed loading of barrels at one of the bunkers into five trucks. The trucks then headed for the Jordanian border.

Israeli intelligence warned Jordan's King Abdullah that WMD was headed for his country. The Jordanians were waiting for the convoy near the border. Inside the trucks were 20 tons of VX liquefied nerve gas and detonation explosives.

Four of the perpetrators were killed in a gun battle and the remaining ten were arrested. They were later identified as al-Qaida members working under the direction of the leader of al-Qaida in Iraq, Abu Musab al-Zarqawi.

Zarqawi had previously expatriated from his own country of Jordan in defiance of the government's cooperation with the west to track al-Qaida. Zarqawi was known to have sent al-Qaida suicide bombers to an Amman urban center that killed dozens of Jordanians in the blast.

A trial of the ten al-Qaida conspirators ensued in May of 2005, revealing that the plan had been to target the prime minister of Jordan, the intelligence headquarters of Jordan

---

[10] Sada, George. *Saddam's Secrets*. Dallas: Integrity Publishers, 2006: 251

and the American Embassy in Jordan. Jordan's King Abdullah said to reporters that, "It was a major operation. It
would have decapitated the government."

The Jordanian press posted various developments in the
trial such as, "Defendants throw shoes in court. Defendants
chant "Allahu akbar" for over a half an hour to disrupt the
court. Defendant, Al-Jayouzi threatens the tribunal with,
"Abu-Musab al-Zarqawi will chop off your heads and stuff
it up your mouths, you God's enemies." In a confession
broadcast on Jordanian television, one of the conspirators
revealed, "In Iraq, I started training in explosives and poi-
sons. I gave all my obedience to Zarqawi." [11]

At the time of the attempted attack, *News Max* reported,
"The Jordan chem-bomb plot was to be executed in three
stages, according to a video re-enactment released by Jordanian officials.

The first stage was to involve a car carrying several al-
Qaida operatives, who would approach the gates of the Jordanian security service in Amman and gun down the facility's armed guards. The car would be quickly followed by a
specially equipped track laden with conventional explosives
that would break through the security service gate and crash
into the main building.

In the third stage, the plot called for three tanker trucks
to follow the breakthrough vehicle, loaded with a combined

---

[11] NewsMax.com, "Jordan WMD Plotter Confesses to Iraqi Involve-
ment," April 27, 2004.

total of 20 tons of chemical weapons laced with conventional explosives. One truck was to crash into the security headquarters, another the U.S. Embassy nearby. A third was to hit a building within a few hundred yards of the other two targets, the Jordanian video showed." [12]

A Jordanian spokesman said, "Had it succeeded, the WMD strike would have been the most deadly terrorist attack in world history, with Jordanian officials estimating that Zarqawi's al-Qaida team could have killed from 20,000 up to 80,000 people."

So President Bush had the same intelligence as the Israelis and was told that the WMD was in Syria soon after our invasion in 2003. But he said nothing as the media pounded away during the 2004 election season that Bush had failed in Iraq because "there was no WMD." The President's insistence upon silence made it possible to save many thousands of lives in Jordan.

Secret U.S. Mission Hauls Uranium Out of Iraq

More recently we get another "leak" out of the media of a similar story about Saddam's nuclear materials. On July 5, 2008, the Associated Press (AP) released a story named, "Secret U.S. Mission Hauls Uranium from Iraq." The story says, "The last remnant of Saddam Hussein's nuclear program – a huge stockpile of concentrated natural uranium –

---

[12] Ibid.

reached a Canadian port Saturday to complete a secret U.S. operation that included a two week airlift from Bagdad and a ship voyage crossing two oceans.

The removal of 550 metric tons of "yellowcake" – the seed material for higher-grade nuclear enrichment – was a significant step toward closing the books on Saddam's nuclear legacy. It also brought relief to U.S. and Iraqi authorities who had worried the cache would reach insurgents or smugglers crossing to Iran to aid its nuclear ambitions"......
"Yellowcake can be enriched for use in reactors and, at higher levels, nuclear weapons using sophisticated equipment. The Iraqi government sold the yellowcake to a Canadian uranium producer, Cameco Corp., in a transaction the official described as worth 'tens of millions of dollars.'....The deal culminated more than a year of intense diplomatic and military initiatives – kept hushed in fear of attacks once the convoys were under way: first carrying 3,500 barrels by road to Bagdad, then on 37 military flights to the Indian Ocean atoll of Diego Garcia and finally aboard a U.S. flagged ship for a 8,500 mile trip to Montreal."

We should all care when our media fabricates stories, such as "Bush Lied," and conceals other facts such as the transfer of WMD out of Iraq.

CHAPTER SIX

JUNK SCIENCE,
GLOBAL WARMING
& CAP AND TRADE

"Once you open a can of worms, it takes a bigger can to re-can them" - Malcolm Forbes

Junk Science has become an industry. The Federal Clean Air Act and Clean Water Act began innocently, but they spawned many hundreds of State, County and autonomous agencies which write their own legislation.

In an effort to make work for themselves and generate new funding these state and local agencies have imposed an overwhelming amount of regulations and fees upon our factories. As a result, our factories began closing in the mid 1990's due to the added cost of a rain of junk science rules and regulations.

The first Air Quality Management District (AQMD) was created in California by a committee formed under State

Speaker Willie Brown. The jurisdiction was to govern all business and residences, except for vehicles, which is the jurisdiction of the Air Resources Board. Naturally, the AQMD sought to regulate factories. However factories only use two sources of power, electricity and natural gas.

Smog is created by autos, trucks, buses and planes, which is the jurisdiction of a different agency. So the AQMD was given jurisdiction over a problem that did not exist. Funding and employment for the AQMD has since driven volumes of make work regulations based on junk science. The by-products of natural gas combustion are carbon dioxide and water, both harmless molecules. But the District determined that trace amounts of nitrogen could be found in natural gas.

Nitrogen combines with oxygen to form various nitrogen oxides, nicknamed NOx. Most of the NOx molecules are harmless, such as nitrogen monoxide, (NO) and nitrous oxide, (N_2O), nicknamed laughing gas. As we might guess, laughing gas is harmless, since we inhale it in the dentist's office.

Nitrogen Monoxide (NO) is naturally produced by our body and facilitates the flow of blood. It is sold as a health supplement to assist blood flow without increasing blood pressure. The AMA's website points out that the FDA, in 1999, approved nitrogen monoxide inhalation therapy for infants with hypertension and certain blood flow issues.

Nitrogen dioxide (NO_2) would cause eye irritation in large enough quantities, but all the oxides of nitrogen together comprise less than $1/1,000^{th}$ of the exhaust from burning natural gas.[1]

For this reason, the Energy Information Administration (EIA) states, "Natural Gas use also is not much of a factor in smog formation."[2]

The National Environmental Trust (NET) states, "Natural gas is becoming an increasingly important fuel in the generation of electricity. As well as providing an efficient, competitively priced fuel for the generation of electricity, the increased use of natural gas allows for the improvement in the emissions profile of the electric generation industry."[3]

Finally, *NaturalGas.org* says, "The use of natural gas does not contribute significantly to smog formation, as it emits low levels of nitrogen oxides, and virtually no particulate matter. For this reason, it can be used to help combat smog formation in those areas where ground level air quality is poor."

But air quality districts have vilified nitrogen oxides and scrambled for reasons to regulate them. Some of their web-

---

[1] Calculated from table in Energy Information Administration, *Natural Gas 1998: Issues and Trends*, pg 58.
[2] Energy Information Administration, *Natural Gas 1998*; Trends and Issues, pg 54.
[3] National Environmental Trust, *Cleaning up Air Pollution from America's Power Plants*," 2002. Issues, pg 54.

sites have called them toxic, which they are not, or even cancer causing carcinogens, which they are not. The sad thing about these useless regulations is that natural gas emissions are truly harmless. We breathe them as we cook over our natural gas range in our kitchens.

Regulations and requirements imposed upon factories by local air quality districts related to natural gas measurement are overwhelming: Required "source testing" to determine the exact weight of the resulting gasses from burning natural gas; natural gas usage reporting; collecting of permit fees for the use of natural gas devices; citations for not reporting properly; sales of energy credits; website reporting software; training classes regarding the rules; hiring of in house consultants to understand the rules; Continuous Emission Monitoring Systems (CEMS) monitoring at the natural gas exhaust; more source testing to compare the natural gas going in and the exhaust coming out, etc.

By 1995, there were 55 Air Quality Districts in California alone and they have spread to nearly all of our counties nationwide.

Cap and Trade.

In 1994, the Los Angeles area AQMD imposed a rule to reduce NOx emissions on the very largest factories in the basin. The rule was called RECLAIM, rule 1146. The list consisted of 466 factories, including a hand full of utilities.

The rule aimed to reduce NOx by 75% from an initial allocation over a five-year period. Each factory was assigned a starting allocation near their current usage.

The District started a trading program whereby factories must buy energy credits to burn more NOx gas than their assigned annual targets, the "Cap and Trade" rule.

Factories that are able to reduce gas below their declining targets can sell energy credits to the AQMD who brokers them to factories who cannot meet the targeted reductions.

The credits were called Reclaim Trading Credits (RTC's). The cost of RTC's went from zero cost to "$154 in 1996, $227 in 1997 and $451 in 1998...in 1999 $4,284... during 2000 $15,377...during 2001, prices for RTC's climbed even higher to over $59,000. At least one trade took place at a price of $62,000." [4]

Many factories were paying roughly $200,000 for their yearly RTC's. The prices were driven up, naturally, by demand for a shrinking supply of credits. Many factories were closing by this time, so the AQMD removed the utilities from the rule to reduce the price of RTC's.

Environmentalists complained that removing the largest users defeated the purpose of the rule. But much economic damage had already been done and is still being done.

---

[4] *An Overview of the Regional Clean Air Incentives Market (RECLAIM), Staff Paper*, by the South Coast Air Quality Management District (SCAQMD), August 14, 2006, Pages, 7&8

By 2004, there were only 311 factories left in the group, down from the original 466.[5] The AQMD's Board Meeting Date: March 2, 2007, Agenda No. 34 states, "The RECLAIM universe consisted of 311 facilities at the end of 2004."

If the factory shuts down all their natural gas boilers, they can sell the resulting trading credits for cash. This aspect of the rule, the cost of reduced production and of the RTC's has caused many of our factories simply to close and sell their equipment.

This brilliant Cap and Trade strategy has been proposed nationally to regulate the next target gas, carbon dioxide. Since the exhaust of natural gas (their only source of heat) is water vapor and carbon dioxide, our factories must comply with Cap and Trade by reducing production.

Not only will this new rule devastate our remaining factories, we are regulating a harmless gas. If we are to regulate a gas, we should regulate a gas that is toxic or one that contributes to smog. We are about to regulate the wrong gas and destroy what remains of our manufacturing base.

A comparable Cap and Trade system to regulate residential heating systems would more aptly be called, "Reduce and Freeze to Death, and Pay While You Do It." Residences burn about one hundred times more natural gas than our fac-

---

[5] Count of 466 from the original RECLAIM NOx Universe of Sources Draft Facility List, 3/31/93.

tories but only factories are regulated.

The Rain of Other Junk Science Regulations.

We have not talked about the regulation of water, both incoming and outgoing (effluent to the sewer).

The national Clean Water Act was intended for drinking water, but State regulators have bastardized it to apply to the effluent that a factory sends to the sewer. The act started by regulating copper in our drinking water to about 40 parts per million. Now our factories have to clean effluent to parts per billion for a variety of metal particulates before they send it to the sewer.

Sanitation districts are required to further clean the effluent resulting in hundreds of millions of dollars of plant upgrades and therefore higher sewer bills for the factories that use the waste lines. Sewer bills for a factory that uses large amounts of water used to be zero, now they are as high as $40,000 per month plus similar previously mentioned reporting, measuring and monitoring costs.[6] Factories even have to capture rainwater off their parking lots, clean it, measure it and pay to put it in the sewer.

The U.C. schools and Cal State Universities are developing new departments and specialized studies for most of these so called environmental issues. So the schools de-

---

[6] Reported to our gas and fluid measurement testing firm by L.A. Dye & Printworks textile mill prior to their closing in 2001.

mand more funding for these new education departments. This brings us to the driving force behind Global Warming.

Global Warming.

Since 1988 when Dr. James Hansen of NASA started the Global Warming scare, a complicit media has sounded the alarm. In 2006, the media all of a sudden started parroting, "The argument is over." But the media simply made that up, the scientific argument is alive and well.

The media has muted the real scientists that almost unanimously oppose the Global Warming crowd, but these scientists can be found by Googling around.

Try for starters, Dr. Richard S. Lindzen, Alfred P. Sloan Professor of Meteorology at Massachusetts Institute of Technology (M.I.T.) who seems to dispute most aspects of Global Warming.

You may remember news sources reporting recently that a "Panel of sixty scientists agree," Global Warming must be addressed and they leapfrogged the scientific argument to discuss various regulatory approaches. This panel of "sixty scientists" was authorized by the United Nations Intergovernmental Panel on Climate Change (IPCC), which is an entirely political body. The summit conference of the "sixty scientists" was carried on CSPAN over a two-day period.

Observable were college professors, not scientists. In fact, the most vocal participant was a Harvard Law professor who was advocating the Cap and Trade method (ring a bell?) to control carbon and another professor who was recommending a flat tax for carbon. No science was discussed.

Some of the participants were members of the "Union of Concerned Scientists." The college degrees of these "scientists" are an eye-opener:

President of the Union of Concerned Scientists is Kevin Knobloch who has a B.S. in Journalism and an M.S. in Public Administration. Executive Director, Kathleen Rest's degrees are an M.S in Public Administration and a PHD in Health Policy. The Director of Science, Peter Frumhoff has a B.A. in Psychology and a PHD in Ecology with experience being a Professor of environmental law at Fletcher School of Law and Professor of Diplomacy at Tufts University, Harvard and University of Maryland. The Director of Strategy is Alden Myer who has a B.S. in Political Science and an M.S. in Human Resources. Beneath Mr. Myer are Media Director, Elliott Negin and four Press Secretaries. That is the Union of Concerned Scientists.

It is environmental organizations such as this that feed the media, who prints anything they say no matter how ridiculous. Some recent statements by groups such as this are, "Epic floods will hit"... "Famine and disease will increase"... "Earth's landscape will transform radically"... "Oceans will rise two feet"... "A quarter of all plants and animals will be at risk of extinction"... and "Scientists speculate that the earth's rotation rate could change." None of their predictions have come true, but their funding grows.

It appears the baton to carry Global Warming has been handed from the media to environmental organizations and college professors who are lining up to reap billions of dollars of funding for new departments and to head those new departments at their university.

At our gas measurement company, we operated a laboratory with technicians licensed by the California Department of Weights and Measures. We certified for accuracy thousands of gas measurement devices.

The science of gas measurement has been refined far beyond what most people know. The custody transfer of gases began in 1834 and the accurate measurement of industrial gases has been defined by the American Gas Association and adopted and regulated by Weights and Measures, a division of the National Institute of Standards and Technology.

Gas measurement experts use four aspects of physics to measure any gas: Pressure, Temperature, Super-compressibility and Specific Gravity.

Specific Gravity should be at the center of any scientific analysis of carbon dioxide warming the atmosphere. Specific Gravity is the ratio of the weight of the subject gas to air. The Specific Gravity of carbon dioxide is 1.52. This means it is over one and a half times heavier than air. It is the same weight as propane (Sp.Gr.1.52). Anyone who uses propane knows it to be an extremely heavy gas.

Carbon dioxide is heavier than the gases that comprise smog. Watch dry ice as the frozen carbon dioxide vaporizes and falls to the floor.

Try an experiment at home. The specific gravity of a fluid is its relationship in weight to water. Weigh some fluids. Log Cabin syrup has a specific gravity of about 1.5, same as carbon dioxide. Slowly pour syrup into a glass of water to get an idea of what carbon dioxide does in air. And any observer can see with his or her own eyes that smog is extremely heavy.

I remember driving in the San Bernardino Mountains near Los Angeles on a hot summer afternoon and was barely able to see the valley floor through the smog, but could see over the top of the smog to Saddleback Mountain, which was approximately 50 miles away. Even our notorious Santa Ana Winds, after blowing all day, are only able to push the smog about six miles out to sea where the smog stops and sits when the winds nod.

The smog is so heavy it can't escape the valley basin and travel to cities in the higher desert. And carbon dioxide? It sits at the bottom of the smog layer. It seeks low points in our storm drains, creek bottoms and sinks into the ground to feed our plants. It is not physically possible for such heavy gases to drift up into the atmosphere and warm the entire atmosphere, much less drift north to the glaciers in the arctic.

Dr. Lindzen of M.I.T. grants that ice core samples from the year 1800 indicate a carbon dioxide level of 275 parts per million (ppm) which is being compared to atmospheric measurements today, of 350 ppm.

Had anyone checked with the AGA or Weights and Measures, they might have been told that carbon dioxide, because it is heavy, seeks low points in the ground and even sinks into the ground like a puddle of water.

So taking a sample from an ice field, which is constantly moving and shifting, would not be accurate. The sample would have to be taken from an absolutely stationary low point.

Even so, comparing an ice core sample to today's atmospheric sample is like comparing bird populations with a sample from a mountaintop two hundred years ago to a sample today taken from the rainforest below. Such a measurement would not stand a chance of being approved by the Department of Weights and Measures.

Consider further that an increase of 75 ppm is only .000075 of our atmosphere. If we assume our atmosphere is about 20,000 feet thick, that is a layer of carbon dioxide that is only 18 inches thick. Even if carbon dioxide were lighter than air and rose up in our atmosphere, such a small amount of gas would have an imperceptible effect on the total temperature.

Have glaciers receded? Yes, in general, but many of the true scientists point out this has been occurring for the past 250 years and is a natural cycle. Proof of this appears on the National Park Service's map of Glacier Bay which shows, by dates, growth of the entire bay from 1790 to 1880. I know nothing about sun related causes, but much has been written about this. Have temperatures risen? Yes, but certainly not because of the heavy gases of carbon dioxide and smog for the former reasons.

Here are the average temperatures per decade recorded by the National Oceanic and Atmospheric Administration.[7]

YEAR	TEMP. F
1900	-
1910	56.52
1920	56.57
1930	56.74
1940	57.00
1950	57.13
1960	57.06
1970	57.05
1980	57.04
1990	57.36
2000	57.64

[7] These temperatures were recorded prior to the manipulation of data. They are not disputed.

Notice the total increase for the last century is 1.12 F but .61 F was before 1950 and the increase since then is less at .51 F. During our greatest industrial and automobile boom from 1950 to 1980 temperatures went down slightly. This is more proof that carbon dioxide and smog have nothing to do with warming. In fact, the fear during that time was global cooling!

Dr. Hansen Contradicts His Own Predictions.

The man who started the whole Global Warming scare, Dr. James Hansen of NASA, noticed an approximate quarter degree jump in temperature over a few years surrounding 1988, (There was a similar jump in temperature surrounding 1934).

Hansen testified before Al Gore's committee and the media spread the fear. But according to Mitch Battros of "Earth Changes Media," there is an old Washington Post story titled "U.S. Scientist Sees New Ice Age Coming," published July 9, 1971. "It told of a prediction by scientist James Hansen and S.I. Rasool of Columbia University, stating the coming ice age is caused by human pollutants."

Then in August 2007 Stephen McIntyre, a Canadian meteorologist, claimed that Dr. Hansen's average annual temperatures from 2000 through 2006 were too high. McIntyre reported this to NASA's Historical Climatology Network (USHCN) and was ignored until he went public with his claim. It wasn't until talk radio shows began announcing the dispute that *NASA admitted they were wrong* and corrected the temperatures in the historical record.

Hansen had been caught in a "mistake" about the temperatures. The correction resulted in a reduction of the average annual temperatures by .15 degrees C, which Hansen claimed was "slight."

However, as any high school student can calculate, .15C is equal to .27F, which is about a quarter of the entire increase in temperature over the last century. Notice that the term changed from Global Warming to "Climate Change."

Global Warming is not the first of the Junk Sciences. It is only the most recent in a fifteen-year litany of junk science legislation.

Having been an industrial real estate agent specializing in the relocation of factories in the 1980's, I can tell you junk science regulation and costs have caused the closure of about two-thirds of all the approximate 1,800 factories that existed in the Los Angeles Basin fifteen years ago.

My specialty was to assist factories to relocate from older expensive buildings near downtown to new larger buildings further out at the same cost, tax deferred. The difference in land price, from about $10 to $2 per square foot, provided enough proceeds to increase the factory size by about 50% from an old metal building to a larger new concrete tilt-up building.

The total sale price matched the purchase price so the transaction cost essentially no cash thanks to a tax deferred 1031 exchange. The new factory would also be closer to their employees who struggled with the difficult commute into the city. Because the factory was in a cleaner environment and brand new, moral went up.

Each year, I was able to assist about 10 small to medium size factories in this manner plus help one or two factories locate into California.

However, by about 1993 factories began closing due to a rain of regulatory costs. There are only about 600 factories left in the Los Angeles Basin. A small number of factories re-located to other states in the 1990's but the same or similar rules have spread nationwide.

Chinese entrepreneurs are the only outsiders smart enough to recognize what is happening. They were aware of our factory closings in the early 1990's because they have always had numerous import/export individuals here to buy for Chinese buyers, parts, equipment or other needed items.

The Chinese observed our factories closing and began making offers for the manufacturing equipment. Kaiser Steel's plant number one foundry was the first to go. The Chinese buyers leased an old motel in San Bernardino for about a year to house their workers. They built a fence around the motel and a bus took them to the Kaiser site every day. They disassembled the metal foundry building as well as the furnaces. It looked like a scrap metal heap for months while they numbered not only each piece of equipment but also the tin metal walls so the old building could be precisely rebuilt.

As rising regulatory costs and the Cap and Trade rule lead to reduced production using natural gas, the factories have two rather obvious options:

1) Due to the Cap and Trade rule, the factory can reap a large cash benefit by simply closing the plant. Since their consumption of natural gas would drop to zero, they can sell the resulting energy credits back to the Air Quality District who brokers the credits to another factory who cannot meet their reduction targets.

2) The factory can respond to multiple offers from Chinese buyers for machinery and equipment. Sometimes the Chinese can buy rights to existing distribution contracts to acquire an existing sales network. But the machinery and ownership of the manufacturing process is shipped to China.

An acquaintance of mine who has been in the machinery moving business for many years recently told me, nothing has changed since the 1990's, "Factories are still closing, the Chinese are buying the machinery and I am shipping the equipment to China."

My cohorts in the industrial real estate market can attest to the dramatic change. As the Chinese have bought our manufacturing equipment they are faced with the problem of exporting the finished product from China into the United States. They began buying or leasing large 500,000 square foot warehouses near the ports of Long Beach and Los Angeles. The vacancy factor for these huge warehouses plunged in the late 1990's from about 9% to less than 2%, a historical low. Then they spilled into the City of Industry and inland to Ontario and even further to 80 miles from the ports, leasing and buying million square foot warehouse buildings as fast as they could be built.

The process consumed most of the remaining large industrial zoned land in the basin. This is the reason for the proposed industrial highway from Mexico into Texas. It is also the reason for the chronic devaluation of the U.S. dollar.

Having solicited and called upon factories in both my careers as an industrial real estate agent and my position with a gas and fluid measurement company, I have intimate knowledge of this subject.

We *need* to reduce smog but it is coming from vehicles, not our factories. I have not seen a factory close for any other reason than costs related to junk science regulation.

Contrary to a myth created by the media, the problem is not that these factories are outsourcing jobs. A factory doesn't hire workers in China when the equipment is here. And think about it, there has always been cheaper labor overseas. Factories would have left decades ago if labor costs were the problem. There have always been international companies that hire overseas. This should not be mistaken for the loss of manufacturing jobs.

Some people have asked, "Why is a factory job so important, they get paid about the same as other workers don't they?"

Imagine a tribe of 100 American Indians. Each Indian makes one pair of moccasins each year as needed, which have a value in wampum of one dollar.

One Indian decides to form a tribal council and ten Indians are elected to serve full time at a pay of one dollar. So now there are only 90 Indians making moccasins with 100 dollars chasing a shortage of 90 moccasins. This causes inflation and the price of moccasins increases. Then one smart Indian decides to start a moccasin factory and he hires four Indians to help him. They manufacture 25 moccasins per year so the tribe produces 110 moccasins and therefore an excess of 10 moccasins.

This does three things: *first*, the price of moccasins goes back down; *second*, the tribe can export, say, 5 moccasins to another tribe, which increases the value of their currency; *third*, the remaining excess of 5 moccasins free 5 Indians from making moccasins so they can start a clothing factory.

The material wealth of the tribe increases dramatically with each new factory. It is not the amount we pay a factory worker, it is the amount of goods that worker produces that adds to the wealth of a nation. Accordingly, it is not the amount we pay a congressman, rather it is the amount that congressman spends that has the opposite affect.

Consider the wealth created in Japan by their manufacture of televisions and automobiles. It happened quickly. All usable wealth in a society is created by manufacturing... all of it.

Our factories are closing, they are not moving and they are not outsourcing the jobs.

Our factories are being driven out of business by junk science environmental costs and regulations.

CHAPTER SEVEN

FROM FIVE ROGUE NATIONS TO ONE

Yes, history repeats itself because we are dumbed down by our media.

The media is silent about the elimination of Rogue Nations.

Conservatives mischaracterize the American media. They correctly accuse the media of being liberal and biased, but they say the media is anti-Bush.

The proper and enduring characterization is that the media is anti-Republican (as well as anti-big business). These two characterizations of the media have held true for at least the last thirty years.

In 1978, Trisha Toyota stuck a microphone into a ten-year-old little girl's face and said, "Aren't you afraid that your next president could start a nuclear war?" The child said, "Yes" as tears of fear filled her eyes.

CBS news had their story and that began the attacks on Ronald Reagan, which did not stop until two years after he left office. The media pounced on the opposite side of every single thing Ronald Reagan tried to do, without exception. Think for a moment, how often would you turn out to be right when all you did was take the opposite stance just to oppose someone?

As it turns out, Reagan was right about every one of the issues of his day and the media was wrong. The media did exactly the same thing to President Bush and the media turned out to be wrong in their accusations once again. The general consensus among liberals, who believe the media, is that the Iraq war was a quagmire and our President's policies failed. But an unbiased look at reality by comparing the before and after of our President's terms reveals a remarkable series of successes.

Not only did the President create two democracies in the heart of the Middle East, which most of us had considered impossible, but he also eliminated four of the five "Rogue Nations."

Prior to our President's aggressions, the United Nations had cited five nations as Rogue Nations that were attempting to acquire nuclear arms and/or weapons of mass destruction with an aggressive or mal-intent.   These nations were: Pakistan, Iraq, Libya, North Korea and Iran.

Upon our invasion of Afghanistan and as a direct result of that invasion, Pakistan admitted and disclosed their entire nuclear weapons program. Furthermore the doctor in charge of the program, Abdul Qadeer Khan, disclosed that they had sold nuclear weapons technology to North Korea and Iran.

As a direct result of our attack on Iraq, Muammar al-Qadhafi disclosed and dismantled his nuclear arms program in Libya.

On Monday December 15, 2003, the day after we found Saddam in the spider hole, Qadhafi called the British Consulate and the President of Italy saying, "I don't want to end up like that." The Libyan leader called to declare that he would disclose his entire nuclear weapons program and discontinue its operation.

After Colin Powell discovered the debacle that Madeline Albright and Jimmy Carter created by agreeing to sell Kim Jung IL stainless steel and other materials to build a "reactor," President Bush's team, led by assistant Secretary of State Christopher Hill, succeeded in 2007 to end the resulting production of plutonium at North Korea's nuclear facility.

Therefore, four of five nations were no longer acting Rogue Nations when the President left office. Only Iran remained as a Rogue Nation. All this was accomplished because we invaded Afghanistan, Iraq and acted as the only country willing to enforce international law.

Perhaps even more remarkable, remember how prior to President Bush 24 million people in Iraq and 16 million in Afghanistan hated us and chanted that we were the great satin?

Now forty million people in Afghanistan and Iraq are freed from oppression, view us as liberators and are grateful to President Bush, thanks to some remarkable leadership by Donald Rumsfeld and our President.

Ronald Reagan's accomplishments were also opposed by the media.

When I heard President Reagan propose the Strategic Defense Initiative (SDI), in his state of the union address, I jumped up, pointed to the television and declared to my wife, "That is the best idea of this century. It will make nuclear war obsolete." The idea of a defense missile that can intercept and destroy an incoming nuclear warhead should end the arms race.

However, the next day a 27-year-old reporter from the New York Times, in an effort to belittle SDI, labeled the program, "Star Wars."

That evening on CBS, Dan Rather squawked Star Wars and the next evening all the other network anchors were squawking Star Wars. Later that week, my Democrat friends on the street were squawking Star Wars.

To me, they sound like a flock of parrots. I learned three things about the media from that experience.

1) The media was pouncing on the opposite side of whatever Reagan proposed, even when the idea was so obviously a good one.

2) When they oppose a Republican idea they do so like a flock of parrots, and Democrats on the street fly with the flock.

3) This is why the media seemed to be not partly wrong on politically charged subjects, but they were seemingly turning out to be totally wrong. The reason was, they were pouncing on the opposite side of Reagan's good ideas simply to oppose him.

Here are some of President Reagan's positions and accomplishments that were opposed by the media.

Reagan recognized the nuclear arms freeze as a ploy by the Soviets, while the media flock led Jimmy Carter to agree with the Soviets regarding their proposed nuclear arms freeze. Presidential candidate Reagan declared that the Soviets were currently in violation of the previous arms treaty.

The media opposed Reagan's tough talk regarding the American hostages that Iran had held captive for fourteen months. The hostages were released on the day before Reagan took office.

Reagan's proposal to follow Milton Friedman's advice to control the money supply to end inflation turned out to be the correct solution. The media had demanded price controls, which Jimmy Carter imposed on credit card rates. The result was to shrink the credit market, which made the situation worse and market rates went even higher to twenty one percent.

Reagan's Strategic Defense Initiative (Star Wars) is currently being requested by a number of countries and test launches from Vandenberg Air Force Base have successfully hit 10 of 11 targets when launched. Early on, the press liked to say the program had failed because only 5 of 9 tests had been successful, but three launches had been scrubbed due to computer glitches.

The media became almost hysterical when Reagan called the Soviet Union an "evil empire." Backed with the proposal of SDI and a rebuilding of the U.S. Navy that Jimmy Carter had severely under-funded, Reagan met with Mikhail Gorbachev in Reykjavik, Iceland in 1986. Reagan confronted Gorbachev and convinced him he could not win the nuclear arms race.

What the media did their best to hide was that Gorbachev asked Reagan to speak on television to the entire Soviet nation. It was this speech, Gorbachev later claimed to David Frost that convinced his nation to give up on the nuclear arms race.

Reagan proposed force, if necessary, as opposed to the media's idea of diplomacy with tyrants such as Muammar al-Qadhafi. Qadhafi was the sole purveyor of international terrorism at the time, including the destruction of commercial airliners and bombing of nightclubs and hotels in Europe. Reagan's surgical missile strike of Qadhafi's terrorist camp, ended Libyan terrorism.

To top it off, Reagan ended the Cold War. He turned out

to be right about confronting communist imperialism with force when he counterattacked the communist takeover of Grenada. Prior to Reagan's presidency one country every two years had fallen to communist imperialism since 1969. The Cold War had loomed for thirty-five years killing millions of innocent people.

The Cold War consisted of seven wars of communist aggression against South Korea, South Viet Nam, Chile, Cambodia, Laos, Nicaragua, Angola, Ethiopia and Grenada.

By the end of his presidency, Reagan was known for cutting spending for the poor. This was simply one more media canard, as explained below.

In November 1980, the previous year budget had been $407 billion. Jimmy Carter lost the election but Democrats passed a proposed budget of $490 billion, a staggering 20.4% increase. Inflation was 12%.

Soon thereafter Reagan proposed a budget of $455 billion with the explanation that it matched inflation, which it did. The media went crazy. They called the $35 billion difference between the Democrat increase in spending and Reagan's proposed increase in spending a "spending cut."

Every weekday afternoon for about a month, House speaker Tip O'Neill would stride out to the Capitol building steps where dozens of network microphones and cameras waited.

Tip would declare such statements as, "Children are

starving in America and yet Ronald Reagan is cutting spending for the poor." The media pounded away with Tip O'Neill's canard for eight years and each year it was not true.

Each year Reagan proposed an increase in social spending but the Democrats proposed a larger increase and the media called the difference a spending cut. Reagan never even proposed to cut social spending. *His budgets proposed increases every year and all categories of social spending increased by an average 9% per year during his tenure.*

The media simply lied about this. In Reagan's book, he says he confronted Tip at a White House function and asked, "Tip, you know those things you say are not true, why do you say them?" Tip put his hand on Reagan's shoulder and said, "Ronnie, it's just politics."

By the end of the 1980's even some Republicans were trying to defend Reagan by saying, "Sure Reagan cut spending for the poor but…"

The power of the media to deceive is nearly total.

CHAPTER EIGHT

THE TWO WARS IN IRAQ

Truths fit together like a 200 piece puzzle, misinformation does not.

Historians and sensible observers need to distinguish that we fought two separate wars in Iraq.

The "War against Saddam in Iraq" was won in forty days when the Iraqis toppled the statue of Saddam. This *first war* accomplished several things:

1. It deposed a fascist and his ability to produce weapons of mass destruction.
2. It helped to create a democracy in the heart of the Middle East.
3. It created an ally from an enemy that previously shot guns in the air and challenged the United Nations.

The *second war* was the "War against al-Qaida in Iraq," which began almost a year later in early 2004 when al-Qaida fighters began to filter into Iraq.

This was the war that the media thought we should fight in Afghanistan. However, bin-Laden and his al-Qaida fighters fled to Pakistan when we defeated the Taliban in Afghanistan.

Had we listened to the media, we would have abandoned Iraq and the country would have crumbled into a state of Sheria run by al-Qaida. Our troops would have moved to Afghanistan to fight the distractions of border skirmishes with the Taliban while al-Qaida won the war against the United States in Iraq.

Our commanders were correct, the war against al-Qaida was in Iraq, not in Afghanistan. The failed policy was that of the Democrat leadership that believed the media and attempted to abandon Iraq to fight in Afghanistan.

According to Mansoor Ijaz, President Clinton's emissary to Sudan, Osama bin-Laden moved to Afghanistan in March of 1996 with five members of al-Qaida. According to State Department estimates, bin-Laden recruited and trained approximately 10,000 al-Qaida fighters over the next five years.

In Iraq, our Marines did not lose a single battle. Al-Qaida fighters did not stand a chance against our Marines. The only way al-Qaida could win or make progress was when we did not fight.

Over the ensuing four years our Marines killed approximately 9,000 al-Qaida fighters in Iraq. By 2007 the life span of an al-Qaida fighter in Iraq had plunged to roughly three months, down from a previous estimate of twenty-nine months.

The war was complicated by Abu-Musab al-Zarqawi, the leader of al-Qaida in Iraq, when he bombed the Shiite Mosque of the Golden Dome on February 22, 2006 in Baghdad.

His obvious plan to "stir the pot" succeeded in turning Iraqi Shiites against Iraqi Sunnis. However, we did not fight the Sunnis or Shiites except to the extent that some morphed into al-Qaida strongholds.

Operating on a tip by Jordanian spies in Iraq to follow Zarqawi's spiritual advisor, Abu-Abdul-Ratman, Major General William Caldwell and Iraqi intelligence found Zarqawi. He was killed by an air strike in Bagouba, Iraq on June 6, 2006.

Using Zarqawi's confiscated laptop, General George Casey and Caldwell planned raids on multiple al-Qaida safe houses where our Marines killed approximately 700 al-Qaida fighters in the next three weeks.

The "War against Al-Qaida in Iraq" was finally won in May of 2008 when U.S. trained Iraqi troops defeated the last stronghold of al-Qaida in Mosul, Iraq. U.S. troops secured Baghdad by September.

The second war in Iraq took four years to win. The accomplishment was to capture and kill roughly 90% of the al-

Qaida fighters that metastasized during the 1990's. The result is that al-Qaida exists as a shell of its former organization, hiding in Wazeristan, unable to travel or communicate except in cognito or by courier.

Critics of President Bush claim he underestimated the length of the war. However in his speech after 9/11, the President said this about the war against al-Qaida,

> *"Now this war will not be like the war against Iraq a decade ago, with a decisive liberation of territory and a swift conclusion. It will not look like the air war above Kosovo two years ago, where no ground troops were used and not a single American was lost in combat. Our response involves far more than instant retaliation and isolated strikes. Americans should not expect one battle, but a lengthy campaign unlike any other we have ever seen. It may include dramatic strikes visible on TV and covert operations secret even in success."*

At the time, the President did not predict that the war against al-Qaida would occur in Iraq but he recognized when it did, as did his commanders in the field. The media and those who believe the media never did figure it out.

CHAPTER NINE

HOW WE BEAT AL QAIDA AND WON THE IRAQ WAR DESPITE THE MEDIA

**We say, "War is not the answer."
However, good came from all of our wars
except the one war we quit.**

Rather than spew media canards about President Bush, his critics should remember what actually happened.

For example, let's review two subjects the media has so distorted that few people are capable of discussing them intelligently. The Iraq war and how should we deal with al-Qaida?

Al-Qaida.

There is no need to be afraid of al-Qaida, but we need to fight them. We cannot ignore the problem and we cannot negotiate with them. The only thing they react to is force.

The good news is that al-Qaida fighters represent such a small percent of the Moslem population that we can mitigate by continuing with the President's plan.

Critics of George W. Bush said that he had no plan to fight al-Qaida. They simply refused to listen or to remember.

One month after 9/11, President Bush and Donald Rumsfeld's remarkably innovative plan was announced in the President's address to the nation:

Paraphrasing and quoting.... This is an enemy that must be fought in three ways:

1. They must be fought in their own land. "...the only way to defeat terrorism as a threat to our way of life is to stop it, eliminate it, and destroy it where it grows."

2. "Therefore, we must have cooperation of the international community and cooperation of leadership in the country where terrorists operate." President Bush called upon all nations to help in this matter. Do you remember now? He said, "Either you are with us or your are with the terrorists." Nearly all nations agreed to help.

3. "We will starve terrorists of funding."

Moslem donations, worldwide, had been funneled to Hamas, PLO, Hezbolah, Taliban and al-Qaida. Yasser Arafat had about $150 million, just in his personal account, not including the money he controlled for Hamas. We know this because his wife claimed it when Arafat died.

Thanks to the bank disclosure legislation of the Patriot Act, the President and 112 other nations that ratified his international plan through the U.N. successfully cut off most of Hamas and nearly all al-Qaida funding by freezing hundreds of bank accounts.

According to the Associated Press (Nov. 9, 2008) approximately 300 Taliban and al-Qaida accounts were frozen. This has worked exceedingly well.

In the months following 9/11, the U.S. and cooperating nations traced approximately 6,000 cell phone calls of al-Qaida operatives in Europe and the United States.

Al-Qaida was using cell phones with a microchip that the Swiss manufacturer had claimed was untraceable. After 9/11, the Swiss company gave us a method to trace these cell calls.

President Bush, the CIA and allies tracked approximately 6,000 cell phone calls using a method devised by the Swiss manufacturer.

Al-Qaida was unaware their phone calls could be traced. Many of the calls were to phones in the United States. The President regularly reported this surveillance to the Senate Foreign Intelligence committee, which continuously approved the surveillance and encouraged it.

It is likely that a senator on that committee leaked this top secret information to editors of the New York Times and Los Angeles Times who reported it after being implored not to do so by President Bush.

As a result, al-Qaida found other ways to communicate.

But in spite of an unsupportive media, three commercial jet-liner hijackings to the United States were prevented as a result of surveillance and efforts of various foreign intelligence agencies. These three British Air flights were bound for New York, Washington, and Los Angeles. Fifteen other attacks upon United States soil have been prevented. Most of these attempted hijackings and bombings were prevented by the tracking of cell phone calls, "chatter" as they were called. Many hundreds and possibly thousands of lives were saved.

On June 23, 2006, the Los Angeles Times and the New York Times disclosed classified details about the President's "Swift" program for tracking finances of al-Qaida operatives.

Again, the information leaked from the Senate Foreign Intelligence Committee. Both newspapers were contacted by the administration and told the information was classified and not to release it. Both editors, Bill Keller of the N.Y. Times and Dean Baquet of the L.A. Times defied the White House's efforts to stop them and ran their stories.

When President Clinton turned down the Sudanese President Umar al-Bashir's offer to extradite Osama bin-Laden for the final time in March of 1996, al-Qaida consisted of Bin-Laden and five men. Clinton's facsimile to President Umar Hassan al-Bashir said, "No, let him go, anywhere but Somalia."

Bin-Laden took with him, Ayman al-Zawahiri, considered by the U.S. to be the planner of the 911 attacks; Mamdouh Mahmud Salim, technical expert; Wadih El-Hage, who planned the embassy bombings in Tanzania and Kenya; Fazul Abdullah Mohammed and Saif Adel.

On May 10, 1996, Bin-Laden and these five men relocated from Sudan to Afghanistan where they built training camps and trained an estimated 10,000 al-Qaida fighters. To date approximately 9,000 of these al-Qaida fighters have been killed or captured in Iraq.

By 2007, the life span of al-Qaida terrorists in Iraq had dropped to about 90 days. President Bush and Donald Rumsfeld's innovative plan worked beyond what anyone could have imagined.

Al-Qaida may be operating at a small fraction of what they used to, but they can grow back like a cancer. And they will, if we let the civil libertarians decide what to do.

President Bush's critics want civil trials for al-Qaida fighters. Madeline Albright told President Clinton to refuse extradition of Bin-Laden because, "We did not feel we had a case against him."

This was after Bin-Laden was known to have bombed the Aden Hotel in Yemen containing one hundred U.S. military officers, bombed the World Trade Center the first time, bombed U.S. marine barracks and training compound in Riyadh, Saudi Arabia and attacked our troops in Mogadishu,

Somalia.

Osama bin-Laden took credit for these acts and yet, Bill Clinton agreed with Ms. Albright and repeated her statement when asked why he refused extradition of Bin-Laden. Regretfully, Clinton and Albright may be right. Our civil courts are likely to free many of Bin-Laden's men.

Critics have not learned President Bush's crucial point that we must allow our military to hold these people as enemy combatants. If the military so decides, the combatants must be tried in military court.

Miranda type civil rights, lack of crime scene investigation, release to custody or jurisdiction, timeliness of release and release with international supervision are all considerations that would be misused or ignored by our civil courts. Releasing these prisoners by any means poses a threat.

Remember that the Israeli's had refused to release the 50 most violent Hamas prisoners when negotiating the Oslo Accords with President Clinton and Yasser Arafat.

The Israeli's had already agreed to release most of the Hamas prisoners, but these prisoners were known to have murdered Israeli citizens.

However, President Clinton sided with Arafat and insisted that all prisoners must be released. As a result, Mohammad Atta was released and subsequently flew an airliner into the World Trade Center.

Nor have critics learned the benefit of Rumsfeld's first

point in his plan. We must fight al-Qaida in their land by assisting local military, using international rules of engagement and military law. This is where the al-Qaida organization grows by teaching boys as young as eight years old to shoot, fight, make bombs and kill infidels.

If our military decides it is safe to release these prisoners it should be to the local military authority where the crimes were committed.

Iraq War.

It was not three months after our 2003 invasion of Iraq that the media decided they should turn against the war, as they did during Vietnam, despite public opinion polls that favored President Bush's plan of action.

The media's comparisons to Vietnam were an obvious stretch, so they quickly switched to a new tack by claiming, "Bush lied."

President Bush said in his January 2003 speech,

"Some have said we must not act until the threat is imminent. Since when have terrorists and tyrants announced their intentions, politely putting us on notice before they strike? If this threat were permitted to fully and suddenly emerge, all actions, all words and all recriminations would come too late. Trusting in the sanity and restraint of Saddam Hussein is not a strategy, and it is not an option."

The canard began when a media source quoted someone as saying that the President said, "Iraq is an imminent threat to us."

Clearly, the President was saying we should not wait for Saddam to become a threat to us.

Then the claim was that President Bush lied about Saddam seeking nuclear material in Niger. He said, "The British Government tells us that Saddam Hussein recently sought significant quantities of uranium from Africa."

That is true, the British Government did tell us that. And to this day, the British say they told us that and furthermore they claim it is true. But the media waged an entire presidential campaign against the Republican president, based on, "Bush lied." He never lied.

In December 2005, Abu-Musab al-Zarqawi (the leader of al-Qaida in Iraq) made a plea to the Moslem world that "we are losing this jihad" (war). "All Moslems must take up arms now, or we will lose."

His plea fell on deaf ears. Most Moslems are peaceful. They saw the power of the U.S. and had no intention of provoking us. Further, most of them were fed up with Zarqawi for his killings of Moslems in Jordan (his own people in his own country) and for blowing up the Golden Shiite Mosque, which started the battle between Shiites and Sunnis. The United States and cooperating foreign intelligence agencies stopped all 18 attempted attacks on U.S. soil and about 100 attacks worldwide after 9/11. There have been only two successful attacks outside the United States, both by Zarqawi, in Jordan and Spain.

The media asked, "What will our out of control cowboy President do next?" The President was not out of control. All three invasions (Kuwait, Afghanistan and Iraq) by Bush Presidents were to enforce U.N. resolutions.

Remember the gulf war in Kuwait? George H.W. Bush drove the Iraqis out of Kuwait. The media and the very same critics repeatedly criticized him for not going all the way to Baghdad to take out Saddam Hussein.

George H.W. Bush waved the U.N. resolution in the air (gesturing) and claiming the resolution did not authorize him to do anything but drive the Iraqi's from Kuwait.

Bush "Jr." acted only on U.N. resolutions, exactly like his father. The U.N.'s resolution for the United States to invade Afghanistan after 9/11 was granted to us without any delay.

After the gulf war, Saddam signed the U.N.'s resolution 1441, agreeing to disclose and dispose of his W.M.D. and to disarm in the presence of U.N. inspectors. Over the next 12 years, Saddam made fools of the United Nations, allowed inspectors to catalog and photograph 17,000 pounds of VX gas, anthrax etc., but then hid these W.M.D., kicked out inspectors, allowed them in again and then kicked them out a second time.

The U.N. added 16 amendments to resolution 1441 allowing Saddam more time. The final two amendments, the 15th and 16th, authorized the use of force! This was the reason we invaded Iraq, not to chase Al-Qaida.

The media later fabricated the notion that Bush had sought al-Qaida in Iraq. (The fact that al-Qaida fighters were drawn to Iraq was a fortunate circumstance because al-Qaida was forced to stand and fight in Iraq).

Bush's notion was that the U.N. had become a paper tiger, weak and ineffective and he was right. To give the paper tiger teeth, President Bush led forty nations who agreed to support him and act by enforcing the 16th amendment of resolution 1441. <u>In all three invasions, the Bush's acted on U.N. resolutions.</u>

But once again less than a year into the war, the media pounced on the opposite side saying the President had no plan for the war.

However, the President's plan and goals were clearly stated:

1. Depose Saddam and his cache of WMD.
2. Create a democracy.
3. Help the Iraqis build an army of about 130,000 troops capable of defending that democracy, (The Iraqi army stands up, we stand down policy).

Then, like a flock of parrots, the media claimed the war

was a failure because we had not found Saddam. Later the flock of media parrots claimed the war was simply a "failed policy" despite the fact that we never lost a battle.

Al-Qaida and the insurgents did not stand a chance against our Marines. To any clear thinking observer who ignored the media, it was obvious the only way we could lose was to retreat as the media demanded. Democrats in Congress who fly with the media flock tried, twice, to cut off funding for the Marines.

With regard to the war being a "failure" and "failed policies," a realistic look at the former goals and accomplishments of our President's effort prove otherwise.

The media has trained our minds to say there was no WMD in Iraq. Really? Saddam killed 105,000 Kurds using Sarin and VX gas. The U.N. inspectors cataloged and photographed the W.M.D. Saddam did have W.M.D. The only intelligent question is, when and where did he hide it?

Thanks to General Sada, Saddam's own Vice-Air Marshall, and various other members of Saddam's army, we know that the W.M.D. was shuttled out of Iraq into three bunkers in Syria during the six-month period prior to our invasion.

But our media would not report this because their goal was to shuttle Bush out of office. After General Sada's disclosure, corroborating evidence from others began to surface in the Israeli and Jordanian press.

Prime minister Ariel Sharon confirmed to the Israeli press that their satellite had tracked the repeated shipments from Iraq to three separate bunkers in Syria and were monitoring the sites via satellite. The Israeli's were silent until they tracked shipments exiting one of the bunkers via a convoy of trucks headed for the Jordanian border.

The Israelis warned the King of Jordan and the convoy was stopped in a shootout at the border. The conspirators were al-Qaida fighters sent by Zarqawi, the leader of al-Qaida in Iraq. The incident made headlines in Jordan as King Abdullah announced the discovery of "enough gas in the trucks to have killed 80,000 Jordanians."

Such a story should make Watergate seem like Dick and Jane, but our media has buried it along with the other accomplishments stated herein.

Iraq President al-Maliki led his army's defeat of insurgents and al-Qaida in Mosul in May of 2008. This was the first victory by the 135,000 strong Iraqi army and represents the beginning of the accomplishment of President Bush's third and final goal.

So lets review President Bush's plan:
1. **Depose Saddam and his cache of WMD, done.**
2. **Create a democracy, done.**
3. **Help the Iraqis build an army capable of defending that democracy, done.**

A keen observer recently compared President Bush and

his loyal followers to King Leonidas and the 300 Spartans.

The other Kings of Greece were misinformed, skeptical, afraid and unwilling to fight, so Leonidas and the 300 stood and fought alone.

King Leonidas and the 300 fought to their deaths while his fellow Greeks refused to help them. In this war, however, Bush won.

It is important to note that prior to Bush's aggressions, the United Nations had cited five nations as "rogue nations" that were attempting to produce nuclear arms and/or weapons of mass destruction with an aggressive or mal-intent. These nations were: Iran, Pakistan, Iraq, Libya and North Korea.

Immediately upon our invasion and rapid defeat of the Taliban in Afghanistan and as a direct result of that invasion, Pakistan admitted and disclosed their entire nuclear weapons program. Furthermore, the Doctor in charge of the program, Dr. Abdul Qadeer Khan, disclosed the fact that he had sold nuclear weapons technology to North Korea and Iran.

Upon our invasion of Iraq and as a direct result of that attack, Muammar al-Qadhafi disclosed and dismantled his nuclear arms program in Libya. On Monday, December 15, 2003, the day after we found Saddam in the spider hole, Qadhafi called the Prime Minister of Italy and the British Consulate to disclose his arms program saying, "I don't want to end up like that."

After Colin Powell discovered the debacle that Madeline Albright and Jimmy Carter created by agreeing to sell Kim Jung Il stainless steel and other materials to build a "reactor," President Bush's team, led by Assistant Secretary of State Christopher Hill, succeeded in 2007 to end the resulting production of plutonium at North Korea's nuclear facility north of Pyongyang.

So four of these five nations were no longer acting rogue nations when President Bush left office. Only Iran remained as a rogue nation. All this has been accomplished because we invaded Afghanistan, Iraq and acted as the only country willing to enforce international law.

Is it any wonder that the Iran hostages were held for fourteen months and then released the day before President Reagan stepped into office?

Is it any wonder that Osama bin-Laden declared war (Jihad) on the United States one month after Bill Clinton was elected President and bombed the World Trade Center the month he took office? Bin-Laden then proceeded to attack us throughout the Clinton administration without a single retaliatory death of his fighters.

It is the fearless nature of our Republican Presidents and their willingness to enforce international law that Al-Qaida and Rogue Nations fear.

"Bringing home the troops" as the media demanded is a signal to al-Qaida that their Jihad is not lost and they are likely to metastasize as they did during the Clinton Administration. Al-Qaida pays remarkably close attention to our election news and history tells us they plan ahead for the next Democrat administration.

Perhaps most important of all, remember how prior to George W. Bush, peoples in Iraq and Afghanistan shot guns in the air and/or chanted that we were the great satin?

Now, people in Afghanistan and Iraq who used to hate us are freed from oppression, view us as liberators and are grateful to President Bush, thanks to some remarkable leadership by our President and Donald Rumsfeld.

Conclusion

The media said Bush had no plan to fight al-Qaida, he did, and it worked. The media said Bush lied, he never lied.

The media revealed classified information about our ability to trace al-Qaida cell phone calls, ruining our effort in that regard.

The media revealed classified information about our ability to trace the flow of terrorist funding, allowing al-Qaida to find alternate methods.

The media buried the fact that Bill Clinton refused extradition of Osama bin-Laden.

The media hides the fact that the U.S. was authorized to use force against Iraq by U.N. Resolution 1441.

The media said President Bush had no plan for the Iraq

War, he did, and it worked.

The media claims there was no WMD in Iraq, there most certainly was.

The media does not mention that President Bush eliminated four of the five rogue nations and turned three of them, plus Afghanistan, into allies.

The media has pounced on the opposite side of whatever President Bush tried to accomplish, just as they did to President Reagan and they have been proven wrong in all cases, once again.

The media trained their adoring public in the U.S. and in Europe to hate Bush. And media puppets do hate Bush, but their hatred was created by the media.

Had a Democrat accomplished what President Bush has accomplished, the media would praise, if not glorify him.

They would praise him for transforming 40 million people in Iraq and Afghanistan from hating the West and calling us the great satin into 40 million people who now call as allies and liberators.

ACKNOWLEDGEMENTS

To acknowledge an instinct is unusual, however it was curiosity that drove me to learn each truth expressed in these chapters. The confusion that is created by our media is the result of their creating and distorting stories to fit their narrow agenda. These distorted stories do not fit with reality and confusion is the result. For me, the confusion was frustrating and curiosity drove the creation of this book. I sometimes wonder if curiosity is not the root force behind motivation. In any event, I thank my parents and God for this driving force.

I am not a reporter or author, but a man off the street who sifted through layers of misinformation collecting tidbits of facts that appeared true by empirical evidence.

Each presumed fact was filed and placed on a table, so to speak, like a two hundred piece puzzle. Over time the pieces that were true fit together to give a picture of reality.

Many of these pieces came from a few truthful and skilled reporters.

Most of the facts brought to light about what caused 9/11 can be found in Richard Miniter's book, *Losing Bin Laden.* He should be commended for being the only reporter among thousands for telling the truth about President Clinton's refusals to accept extradition of Osama bin-Laden. Ronald Kessler's book, *The Terrorist Watch*, is a perfect complement to the former, with its scrupulous account of President Bush's successful approach to fighting terror. Not just Americans but all should read these books.

Thanks to Mansoor Ijaz for his valuable information and effort to help our country. One can only wish that the Clinton Administration had acted upon it. General Georges Sada and his book, *Saddam's Secrets*, is the only account of what happened to the WMD that fits with other evidence.

Thank you to my editor, Cherie Smith, for her thoughts and restructuring of the book. She even inspired me to write a new chapter regarding Social Security. Thank you to my father, Bob Moodey, without whom I would not have completed this book and for his life-long insight. Finally thank you to my wife, Christie, for all her feedback, corrections and advice.

A Time for Truth, 14
Abdullah, King, Jordan, 63-64, 110
Adel, Saif, 50, 104
Aden Hotel, 30, 32, 46, 103
Afghanistan, 31, 49, 88-90, 96, 103,
  107, 111-114
Albania, 43
Al-Bashir, Omar Hassan, Sudan
  President, 31, 48-50, 102
Albright, Madeline, 48, 56, 89,
  103-104, 111
Al-Jayouzi, 64
Al-Maliki, Nouri, Iraqi President, 110
Al-Qaida fighters, 10,000 trained,
  31-32, 49, 104, killed 103
Al-Qaida, 31-32, 38, 41, 43, 56, 63,
  95-106, 108, 110, 113
Angola, 93
AQMD, Air Quality Management
  District, 67-72, 83
Arafat, Yasser, 47, 100, 104
Assad, President Bashir al- (Syria),
  59-60
Atta, Mohammed, 33, 46, 50-51, 53,
  56, 104
Baghdad, Iraq, 97
Bali nightclub bombing, 43
Baquet, Dean, 5, 102
Berger, Sandy, 48-49, 52-54, 56
Bernstein, Carl, 6
Bin-Laden, Osama, 11, 30-32, 35,
  46-52, 54, 56, 96, 104-105, 112-113
Bosnia, Yugoslavia, 43
Brown, Willie, 68
Budgets, U.S., 93-94
Bush lied, (he did not), 105
Bush, George H.W., 107
Caldwell, General William, 97
Cambodia, 93
Cap and Trade, (RECLAIM Rule),
  70-72, 75, 83
Carbon dioxide, 72, 75-78
Carney, Timothy, Sudan Ambassador,
  48
Carter, Jimmie, 89, 91-92, 112
Casey, General George, 97
CBS News, 10, 87
Cell phone calls, Chatter, 101-102
Chemical Ali, Ali Hussein al-Majid, 60

Chemical companies, 7
Chile, Chilean government, 26-28, 93
China, Chinese, 82-85
Christopher, Warren, 47
Clean Air Act, 67
Clean Water Act, 67, 73
Clinton, Bill, 11, 30-32, 34, 45-56, 96,
  102-104, 113
Cold War, 92-93
Dies, Bob, 36
Dow Jones averges, 15-16
EIA, Energy Information
  Administration, 69
Elder, Larry, 60
El-Hage, Wadih, 50, 103
Embassy bombings, 103
Erwa, General Elfatih, 48
Ethiopia, 93
Extradition offers, 11, 30-31, 48-49,
  52-56, 104
Factories, decline of, 68, 70-73, 81-86
FISA, Foreign Intelligence Surveillance
  Act, 32-33, 36, 47
Fort Dix Army Post, 44
Fox News, 51
France, 58
Freeh, Louis, 34-35
Friedman, Milton, 26, 91
Gellman, Barton, 54
Glacier Bay, 79
Global Warming, 74, 76, 80-81
Goldberg, Bernard, 10
Golden Shiite Mosque, 97, 106
Gorbachev, Mikhail, 92
Gore, Al, 80
Gorelick, Jaime, 34, 45, 47, 52-53, 56
Great Society, The, 13
Grenada, 93
Guantanamo Bay prison, 41-44
Hamas, 31, 46, 49, 101, 104
Hammer, Armand, 9, 10
Hannity, Sean, 5, 51-52, 55
Hansen, James, 74, 80-81
Hezbollah, 31, 49, 100
Hill, Christopher, 89, 112
Hussein, Saddam, 57-61, 65, 95,
  105-111
Iceland, Reykjavik, 92
Ijaz, Mansoor, 31, 49-50, 56, 96

Il, Kim Jung, 89, 112
Insight Magazine, 61
Investors Business Daily, 28
IPCC, Intergovernmental Panel on
  Climate Change, 74
Iran hostages, 112
Iran, 88-89, 91, 111-112
Iraq, 57, 60, 62-66, 88-90, 95-99,
  103, 105, 107-114
Islamic Jihad of Egypt, 31, 49
Israel, 31, 33, 46-47, 61-63, 104,
  110
Japan, 86
Jordan, Amman, 63-65, 97, 107,
  109-110
Kahn, Dr. Abdul, 89, 111
Kaiser Steel, 82
Keller, Bill, 5, 102
Kennedy, Weldon, 34
Kenya, Nairobi Embassy, 32, 50,
  103
Kessler, Ronald, 29, 32-36
Kurds, Iraq, 109
Kuwait, 107
Laos, 93
Leonidas, King, 111
Libya, 9, 88, 111
Limbaugh, Rush, 47, 52
Lindzen, Dr. Richard, 74, 78
Loftus, John, 60-61
Los Angeles Times, 5, 8, 10,
  101-102
Losing Bin-Laden, 45, 51
McIntyre, Stephen, climatology
  mathematician, 80
Medicare, 16, 24
Middle East Quarterly, 62
Miniter, Richard, 45, 51-52, 55
Mogadishu, Somalia, 30, 46, 103
Mohammed, Fazul, 50, 104
Mosul, Iraq, 97, 110
Mueller, Robert, Director of FBI,
  35-36
NASA, 74, 80-81
National Oceanic and Atmospheric
  Administration, 79
National Park Service, 79
Naturalgas.org, 69

NCTC, National Counter-terrorism
  Center, 39-41
NET, National Environmental Trust,
  69
New York Times, 5, 10, 90, 101-102
News Max, 55, 64
Nicaragua, 93
Niger, Africa, 106
9/11 bombers, Mohamed Atta and
  Marwan al-Shehhi, 50
9/11 Commision, 9/11, 51-56,
  100-101
North Korea, 88-89, 111-112
Nuclear arms race, 92
Nuclear materials in Iraq, 65-66
Occidental Petroleum, 9
Oil crisis, 2, 8-10
O'Neill, Tip, 93-94
OPEC, 8, 9
Oslo Agreement, 47, 104
Pakistan, 41, 88, 96, 111
Palestinians, PLO, 31, 49, 100
Path to 9/11, 53
Patriot Act, 37-38, 100
Pinera, Jose, 26-27
Plan for Iraq War, 102, 108, 110
Plan to fight al-Qaida, 100-102
Poor, the, poverty, 14-15, 27-28
Powell, Colin, 52, 89, 112
Pyongyang, 112
Qadhafi, Muammar al-, 8, 89, 92, 111
Rather, Dan, 10, 90
Ratman, Abu-Abdul, 97
Reagan, Ronald, 10, 11, 13, 28, 88,
  90-94, 112, 114
Redd, John Scott, NCTC, 39, 41
Resolution 1441, 58, 108, 113
Resolution, Gulf war, 58, 107
Rice, Susan, 49
Rockefeller, Jay, 51, 55
Rogue Nations, 87-89, 111-112, 114
Rosslyn Hotel, 54
RTC's, RECLAIM Trading Credits, 71
Rumsfeld, Donald, 37-38, 90, 100,
  103-104, 113
Sada, General Georges, 57, 59-62,
  109
Saddam's Secrets, 57

Salim, Mamdouh, 50, 103
Sarin gas, 61, 109
Saudi Arabia, Riyadh, 30, 48, 103
Savage, Michael, 45, 53
Scruggs, Richard, 33-34
SDI, Strategic Defense Initiative, 10, 90-91
Sharon, Ariel, 62, 110
Shehhi, Marwan al-, 50
Sheria, 96
Shiites, 97, 106
Simon, William, 14
60 Minutes, 6
Smog, 77, 80
Social Security, 15-28
Somalia, 30-31, 46, 49, 102
South Korea, 93
South Vietnam, 93, 102
Soviet Union, 91-91
Spain, 107
Spartans, 300, 111
Specific gravity, 76-77
Star Wars, 10, 90-91
Sudan, 31, 48-50, 54, 96, 104
Sunnis, 97, 106
Supermax ADX prison, 42
Swiss manufacturer of cell phones, 101
Syria, 57-62, 65, 110
Taha, Ali, Sudan foreign minister, 48
Taliban, 96, 100-111, 111
Tanzania, Dar-es-Salaam Embassy, 32, 50, 103
Taxes, income, 13-14
Tenet, George, CIA, 35-36
Terrorists, attempted attacks, 41-44:
 Abu Zubaydah,
 Abdullah al-Muhajir,
 Binyam Muhammad,
 Ramsey Yousef,
 Khalid Sheikh Mohammed (KSM),
 Riduan Hambali,
 Majid Kahn,
 Talib Shareef,
 Mohamad Shnewer,
 Argon Abdullahhu,
 Duka brothers,
 Serdar Tatar,

 Hassem Hammoud,
 Hamid Hayat
The Terrorist Watch, 29
TIDE, Terrorist Information Datamart Environment, 39-40
Timmerman, Kenneth, 61-62
Toyota, Trisha, 87
Trade balance, 82-86
Turabi, Hassan, 31, 50
U.S. Dollar decline, 84-86
Union of Concerned Scientists, 75:
 Kathleen Rest,
 Kevin Knobloch,
 Peter Frumhoff,
 Alden Myer,
 Elliott Negin
United Nations, 58, 88, 95, 101, 108-109, 111
USS Cole, 32, 50
Vandenberg AFB, 92
Vietnam, 105
VX gas, 61, 63, 107, 109
Wall, The, 33-34, 38, 47
Washington Post, 54, 80
Watergate, 6
Wazeristan, Pakistan, 97
Wealth of a nation, 84-86
WMD, Weapons of Mass Destruction, 57-59, 61-63, 65, 95, 107-110, 114
Woodward, Bob, 6
Woolsey, James, 32
World Trade Center, 30, 32-33, 45-49, 54, 56, 103-104, 112
Yaalon, Lt. General Moshe, 61
Yemen, 30, 32, 41, 46, 105
Yousef, Ramsey, 46
Yugoslavia, (former), 43
Zarqawi, Abu Musab al-, 63, 65, 97, 106-107, 110
Zawahiri, Ayman al-, 50, 103